GREAT WAR BRITAIN
MIDDLESBROUGH
Remembering 1914–18

GREAT WAR BRITAIN

MIDDLESBROUGH

Remembering 1914–18

PAUL MENZIES

IN ASSOCIATION WITH THE DORMAN MUSEUM

The History Press

I would like to dedicate this book to my late father, who sadly died during the writing of this book, and to all those from Middlesbrough who experienced the Great War a century ago.

And to my wife, Jackie.

First published 2014

The History Press
The Mill, Brimscombe Port
Stroud, Gloucestershire, GL5 2QG
www.thehistorypress.co.uk

British Library Cataloguing in Publication Data.
A catalogue record for this book is available from the British Library.

ISBN 978 0 7524 9971 0

Typesetting and origination by The History Press
Printed in Great Britain

CONTENTS

TIMELINE

1914

4 August

Great Britain declares war on Germany

28 August

First meeting of Middlesbrough Recruiting Committee

17 September

First wounded soldiers arrive at Hemlington Hospital

16 December

Middlesbrough defences strengthened after bombardment of Hartlepool

28 June

Assassination of Archduke Franz Ferdinand in Sarajevo

23 August

Battle of Tannenberg commences

6 September

First Battle of the Marne

19 October

First Battle of Ypres

1915

25 April

Allied landing at Gallipoli

31 May

First German Zeppelin raid on London

20 December

Allies finish their evacuation of and withdrawal from Gallipoli

6 January

The Tees-side Battalion is officially raised at Middlesbrough Town Hall

7 May

Germans torpedo and sink the Lusitania

22 July

Middlesbrough Football Club officially closes for duration of the war

1916

24 January

*The British Government
introduces conscription*

21 February

Battle of Verdun commences

10 March

*First Military Tribunal at Middlesbrough
hears 400 cases of exemption*

31 May

Battle of Jutland

4 June

Brusilov Offensive commences

1 July

*First day of the Battle of the Somme
with 57,000 British casualties*

27 August

Italy declares war on Germany

27 November

Zeppelin L34 shot down over Tees Bay

18 December

Battle of Verdun ends

1917

6 April

*The United States declares
war on Germany*

9 April

Battle of Arras

31 July

Third Battle of Ypres (Passchendaele)

13 August

*Middlesbrough Food Committee
formed – will issue ration books*

20 August

Third Battle of Verdun

26 October

Second Battle of Passchendaele

20 November

Battle of Cambrai

7 December

USA declares war on Austria–Hungary

1918

13 January

Middlesbrough Tank Week begins

3 March

Russia and the Central Powers sign the Treaty of Brest–Litovsk

21 March

Second Battle of the Somme

28 June

Tees-side Battalion ceases to exist

15 July

Second Battle of the Marne

8 August

Battle of Amiens, first stage of the Hundred Days Offensive

22 September

The Great Allied Balkan victory

27 September

Storming of the Hindenburg Line

8 November

Armistice negotiations commence

9 November

Kaiser Wilhelm II abdicates, Germany is declared a Republic

11 November

Armistice Day, cessation of hostilities on the Western Front

PREFACE

For more than 100 years the Dorman Museum has been central to Middlesbrough's commemoration of those people from, or associated with, the town who made the ultimate sacrifice in the terrible wars of the twentieth and twenty-first centuries.

The museum was officially opened on 1 July 1904, by the colonel-in-chief of the Yorkshire Regiment, as the 'Dorman Memorial Museum'. It was presented to the town by Sir Arthur Dorman as a memorial to his son, George Lockwood Dorman, and others of the Yorkshire Regiment who lost their lives during the South African or Boer Wars of 1899–1902. It is one of Middlesbrough's landmarks, and stands alongside the cenotaph, and the associated wall that was originally erected in 1922 as the Middlesbrough war memorial to those who fought and died in the First World War. It was rededicated to include those from the Second World War and later conflicts.

Housed inside are collections that include material representative of the townspeople's experiences of war, both on the home front and the front line; from photographs and letters, military equipment and munitions, medals and commemorative items, to souvenirs and mementos. These artefacts, along with Middlesbrough Council's collections held by its library service and the joint service, Teesside Archives, which it manages on behalf of its Tees Valley partners, and material that the local community have shared and made available, are central to our study and understanding of the past.

Now part of Middlesbrough Council's Cultural Services Section, the Dorman Museum has enjoyed supporting author Paul Menzies in his research and writing of this important new publication about Middlesbrough's Great War effort, and is grateful to the publishers, the History Press, to be selected as the official launch venue for the book. *Great War Britain: Middlesbrough* contains a wealth of material and stories, much of it told for the first time, and is a fitting tribute to the courage and resilience of the town's people, in this important centenary anniversary of the start of the 'War to end all wars'.

Phil Philo
Senior Curator, the Dorman Museum, 2014
www.dormanmuseum.co.uk

FOREWORD

The author has done great service in writing this account of life in Middlesbrough during the First World War. This book takes its place alongside the other excellent local history publications by Paul Menzies. His detailed research into the First World War gives us a fascinating glimpse into wartime life in the 'Boro'. Many of the stories are appearing here in print for the first time.

We learn that, along with the grit and determination, went the hardship and suffering, alleviated in part by the numerous voluntary relief organisations.

Crathorne Hall, south of Middlesbrough, operated as a British Red Cross hospital from 13 November 1914 to 9 July 1917. A total of 423 men were patients there, under the command of Mrs J.L. Dugdale, most men being sent from the military hospital in Newcastle. The Dugdale family met all of the expenses incurred in running the hospital. (Courtesy of The Lord Crathorne)

After conscription started in January 1916 the role of women became even more crucial, particularly in the munitions factories. Their heroic efforts transformed women's lives for ever.

There was a fighting spirit in the town, encouraged and promoted by the mayor and countless others. Schoolchildren helped the war effort by making sandbags; women knitted stockings for 'our boys at the Front'; there were numerous fundraising efforts of all kinds.

As mentioned in the book, Crathorne, where I live, played its part with regular voluntary donations from the workers on the estate to 'The Prince of Wales National Relief Fund' and there was a VAD (Voluntary Aid Detachment) hospital run by my grandmother, Violet Dugdale. Her son Thomas (my father) went to the Front as a young officer in 1917, and she wrote to him there every day. Along with every other mother writing to a son at the Front, she did not know whether her next letter would be the last he ever received.

Over 3,000 men from Middlesbrough died in the conflict, and as we read through the following pages we remember them and their families, and the ultimate sacrifice they made during the Great War.

The Lord Crathorne KCVO
2014

INTRODUCTION AND ACKNOWLEDGEMENTS

No man has greater love or self-control
Than he who gives his life for that of friend
This he has done and captain of his soul
Played gamely – to the end

An extract from a dedication written
for the burial of George Hutton Bowes-Wilson, 1/4th Battalion
Alexandra, Princess of Wales' Own Yorkshire Regiment

The personal journey I have taken when writing this book has stretched from a childhood listening to the Great War experiences of older relatives, to my journey to the Western Front last year. Whilst this was for the purpose of research, I also wanted to be able to hold my hands up and say that I had followed in the footsteps of the soldiers 100 years ago. I knew I would have felt uncomfortable writing a book on the Great War, and Middlesbrough, had I not done so.

The most remarkable discovery in my research has been the sheer enormity of the subject in every way. The thousands of graves and names on memorials like the Menin Gate in Ypres, and standing at the grave of the young Middlesbrough footballer, Harry Cook, were both very moving. The beautiful windswept landscape of the Somme seemed so far away from the world he knew as a teacher in North Ormesby, yet as I placed a wooden cross next to his white gravestone, I was the link for a few moments across time and space, between 1917 when he died and today.

Enormity is a word that describes the Great War in every way. Over 3,000 names are on the memorial tablets at Albert Park and, as I discovered, there is an increasing amount of material about the war. When writing a book of this genre there are some key decisions to make before you put pen to paper. For me, it was the choice of approach; I wanted to bring some insight into the lives of those who were here in Middlesbrough, so this is not a military history of the war, and there is not a great deal about battles. Instead this is a detailed history of what it may have felt like for people living in the town at that time. I have tried to cover as many topics as possible, focusing on some that would not normally draw much attention from local historians.

I must apologise to any of the numerous people that I have met in the course of the last three years if I have not included the name of their family member. Space has been very tight in this book, and I have had to restrict named people to those who furthered the story at that point. I have been shown extraordinary kindness by the many people who have helped me out during my research, and it has been a pleasure to have worked with them. I thank them all.

In particular I want to thank Phil Philo and his staff (Louise Harrison, Gill Moore and Jenny Philips) at The Dorman and Captain Cook Birthplace Museums for their constant encouragement and help. Paul Delplanque of the *Evening Gazette*, until his recent retirement, has been incredibly patient with me as I kept on asking for more and more material. The staff at Teesside Archives – Kimberley Starkie and Corrie Dales in particular have been outstanding in their support, under the guiding hand of Ruth Hobbins. Jenny Parker, at Middlesbrough Reference Library, has been a huge help, and allowed me to access material, often at short notice. Middlesbrough Football Club, too, have been superb – I must mention Jo-Ann Swinnerton who made it all possible, and Diane O'Connell and Graham Bell for giving their time.

I also thank those who shared information on their family, particularly those who came to the library event in

November 2013 – it was so good to talk to you. Even if I have not used your material directly, it proved useful in building up a picture of the world as it was then. I would like to thank Joe Pearson, the descendants of J. Briggs, and finally, Jean Brighton. Also Georgina Hustler, Alice Barrigan, Pauline Weatherly and Sandra Morgan – all of whom gave me a lot of time. I also wish to thank Alan McKinnell for all his support.

Thanks to Jonathan Swingler, Mike Hill, Alastair Brownlie and Mike Parr at BBC Tees – all have taken a great interest in the book, and I have been fortunate enough to make some recordings for the BBC World War One website about life in Middlesbrough at that time. In particular I would like to thank John Foster of BBC Tees who worked tirelessly with me on my radio series on Middlesbrough 1914, broadcast in July and August 2014. His energy and support was wonderful. The History Press too has been excellent, and very patient – thank you, Matilda Richards and Rachel Jewitt.

Finally, I want to thank people in my other working roles, for their support and interest, particularly colleagues at Yarm School including David Dunn, Janice Nickson and Norma Brown. Also Carol, who with a coffee and a smile has kept me going on some tough days. My heartfelt thanks must also go to my wife Jackie, who, like the people left behind in 1914, has shouldered a huge burden but been of great support.

I have tried to check all facts in this book and take full responsibility for any errors. If you would like to email me at m.menzies1@ntlworld.com I will try my best to correct it. Similarly I have tried to acknowledge all material in the bibliography, but my apologies if I have missed anyone.

Paul Menzies
May 2014

MIDDLESBROUGH, 1914

There were those still alive, in 1914, with memories of Middlesbrough from almost a century before, a time preceding the building of the Victorian town, when Middlesbrough Farm stood alone on raised land close to the River Tees.

A purpose-built town, Middlesbrough was a shipping port for the export of coal from the Durham coalfields, and by 1914 it was renowned for its iron and steel and ship building industries.

There was a predominantly male population in 1914, totalling 126,452, most of whom were employed in heavy industry. With few opportunities for women outside the retail trade or domestic service, many found themselves confined to the home.

Most working people lived in terraced streets stretching southwards from the river, a pattern that marked the town's growth from tiny hamlet to county borough. In the immediate pre-war years new suburban areas were established and were favoured by those with greater financial means.

Many Middlesbrough men spent their days toiling away in heavy industry in scenes like this one from the local ironworks. (Author's collection)

1

A Summer Storm

The New Bowling Green

For almost fifty years Albert Park had been the pride and joy of the citizens of Middlesbrough. Now, on a hot day in July 1914 it was to have a new bowling green, created under the watchful eye of Councillor George Bowes-Wilson, chairman of the Park Committee. This was an important day, the climax of two years' work. With a darkening sky and ominous rumblings of distant thunder he prayed for the storm to pass by.

His prayers were answered and, minutes later, he was smiling at his 2-year-old son, Maurice, presenting the mayor's wife, Mary Bruce, with a 'handsome bouquet of pink carnations'. With barely any time to spare, special guest Mrs H.F.W. Bolckow performed the opening ceremony, before the fierce storm scattered the crowd. The dignitaries retired to the shelter of a large marquee, where Bowes-Wilson and his wife entertained them to tea; outside the crowds rushed to find shelter in the cafés and public houses on Linthorpe Road.

Like many summer storms, this one was short lived, but in hindsight it was a portent of what was to come. The opening of the bowling green was one of the last municipal ceremonies in the town before the war. Within a year, Bowes-Wilson and his son would be dead; little Maurice died suddenly on 16 March 1915,

George Bowes-Wilson 1878–1915, a Middlesbrough solicitor and a member of Middlesbrough Borough Council (Exchange Ward). (Courtesy of Middlesbrough Council)

Middlesbrough mayor, W.J. Bruce, who was in office at the start of the war, is remembered for his war work. Among many other duties he led the town's remarkable recruitment drive. (Courtesy of the Dorman Museum)

and only three months later his father George died too, on a battlefield near Ypres in Belgium. When Bowes-Wilson's young wife thanked the town council for their condolences, she wrote: 'all seems very black and hopeless to me now ... [but I] hope the bowling green, my husband's final undertaking for the council before enlisting, will be a lasting memorial of his work.'

Three weeks later, the contents of their home were auctioned off at J.S. Storry's Salerooms in Newport Road – a home and a family ruined. Many local families would suffer a similar experience, with feelings of bleak despair in the coming years of war.

Archduke Who?

The assassination of Archduke Franz Ferdinand and his wife, Sophie, in Sarajevo the previous Sunday, 28 June, raised no more than passing interest in the town. Even those who knew where the Balkans were generally agreed they were too far away to be of any real concern. The *North-Eastern Daily Gazette*'s editorial summed it up: managing 'Foreign Affairs' could be a problem but the recent agreement with Germany over Mesopotamia was surely 'a step towards a better understanding in Europe'. Besides, the situation over home rule in Ireland had recently become more threatening, with the Teesside United Irish League now calling for the formation of a local corps of Irish National Volunteers.

With the ending of the school year came the formalities of Speech Day. On Wednesday, 22 July 1914, Lady Sadler, watched by the mayor, presented the prizes at Kirby School, where the increasing breadth of the curriculum was particularly praised. Two days later, Middlesbrough High School's 44th Annual Speech Day, chaired by Sir Hugh Bell Bt, took place in front of a large crowd at the Town Hall. The headmaster of the Boys' School since 1901, William Edwards, and headmistress at the

Graham's Yard, one of the many areas of slum housing and poverty in pre-1914 Middlesbrough. (Courtesy of Middlesbrough Reference Library)

Life was tough for many families in these filthy decrepit living conditions, many of which had been condemned several years before 1914. (Courtesy of Middlesbrough Reference Library)

Girls' School since 1893, Gertrude M. Bedford, both praised the excellent results achieved by their pupils.

The situation in Ireland unfortunately kept the guest of honour, the Right Honourable Joseph A. Pease MP, President of the Board of Education, in London. His under-secretary, C.P. Trevelyan, was a popular replacement, promoting in his speech the ideology of education, and advising parents to send their children to school as 'early as you can [and] above all, keep them there as long as you can'.

This speech day, the final school event before the war, would later be sadly recalled. Some of the boys in the audience that day would soon be going to fight for king and country. It would fall to William Edwards, a few years later, to lead the school in very different circumstances, a poignant gathering to honour more than 700 High School old boys who had joined up – of whom 111 never returned.

Trevelyan's speech made no reference to events in Europe yet, less than two weeks later, Britain would be at war. On Thursday, 23 July 1914, the home rule crisis in Ireland continued to over-shadow developments in Europe, with the *North-Eastern Daily Gazette* devoting only four paragraphs to the ultimatum issued by Austria–Hungary to Serbia, or was it 'Servia'? (The newspapers still couldn't seem to decide which spelling to use.)

On Saturday, 25 July 1914, Middlesbrough thrilled to the news that their swimming hero, Jack Hatfield, had retained the national long distance swimming championship, over a 5 mile course on the Thames from the Anglian Boathouse at Kew to Putney Pier. Local summer shows attracted good crowds. Meanwhile, elsewhere, Serbia accepted all but one of the conditions of Austria–Hungary's ultimatum, and Austria–Hungary rejected this response by closing its embassy in Serbia. It was a curious juxta-position – two different worlds, the normality of local day-to-day life continuing alongside events which were changing history.

Middlesbrough High School was one of the town's leading schools; 111 former pupils were to lose their lives in the war, a fact commemorated in a memorial plaque, which still exists today. (Courtesy of Teesside Archives)

Civil war appeared even closer, after a disturbance in Dublin on Sunday, 26 July 1914, ended in terrible bloodshed, with three people killed and sixty injured. Yet with Austria–Hungary seemingly intent on going to war with Serbia, the European crisis was causing concern too. A cabinet meeting, on the morning of Monday, 27 July 1914, focused for the first time on Europe. With Serbia certain to seek (and receive) support from Russia, both France and Germany would almost certainly be dragged into the affray, an escalation with serious implications for Britain.

The press, with their political allegiances, was an influential power. Middlesbrough's daily newspaper, the *North-Eastern Daily Gazette*, had a circulation of over 70,000 copies. Aware of the potential economic effects of war on local businesses due to reliance on foreign orders, the newspaper was a staunch supporter of the Liberal government's desire to avoid conflict. Nevertheless, events in Europe were increasingly impossible to ignore. When Sir Maurice William Ernest de Bunsen, the British Ambassador to Austria, telegraphed Edward Grey from Vienna on Tuesday, 28 July that Austria-Hungary had invaded Serbia, the *North-Eastern Daily Gazette* was forced to run the headline 'Austrians March on Belgrade' – announcing special arrangements had been made 'for receiving the latest telegrams of the hostilities now taking place between AUSTRIA AND SERVIA (sic)'. Although there was no particular support in Middlesbrough for Austria-Hungary, or for Serbia, there was a feeling of moral injustice over this confrontation and the *Gazette* was determined to keep readers informed.

High on the government's agenda was safeguarding national security. Over the next few days several instructions from the government's 'War Book', a range of 'precautionary measures', were carried out. This lengthy document, put together by the Committee of Imperial Defence in 1907, contained precise details of the steps to be taken by each department in a time of grave emergency. With secrecy an important factor, the press were asked not to report any further facts about either ship or troop movements.

The Garden Fete

Against this backdrop, Sir A.J. Dorman hosted a 'Grand Bazaar and Garden Fete' at his home, Grey Towers, on Wednesday,

29 July 1914, to help raise funds for the new church at Nunthorpe. Imperial Tramways ran a special timetable, with a special fare of only 6*d* (2p) and buses leaving the town every hour during the afternoon. Opened by the Marchioness of Zetland, the fete was a great success with large crowds, and Sir Arthur, who had already donated a site for the new church, was so delighted that he gave a further £1,000. The darkening shadow of national affairs, however, meant the town's Liberal MP, Penry Williams, was unable to get back to Middlesbrough to open the Grove Hill Allotment Show, having to remain in London while his wife took his place.

Wednesday's eye-catching headline, 'War: All Europe Arming', alerted readers to a seemingly deteriorating situation. With a presentation style that would become increasingly familiar over the next four years, the *North-Eastern Daily Gazette* offered in-depth information on the situation, aided by a detailed map.

By Thursday, 30 July 1914, the situation in Ireland was no longer making the main headlines; those fighting for home rule agreed that priority must be given to the national interest, removing, for the time being at least, any imminent threat of civil war. After Great Britain's declaration to Germany that it might not remain neutral if the situation escalated, the question now being asked was 'Shall England have to fight?'

The Middlesbrough public were becoming more informed. The regular newspaper boys on the corner of Marton Road taunted each other by yelling, with increasing noise, 'War declared between Austria and Serbia!' When the situation came to blows, scattering placards and newspapers everywhere, one customer remarked, 'just like Austria and Serbia – fighting over nothing!'

On Friday, 31 July 1914, as rumours of war became more persistent, an already 'jittery' London Stock Exchange failed to open. The Bank of England, anticipating financial panic, increased the bank rate from 4 to 8 per cent, the highest rate since November 1873 (it would be 10 per cent the following day). Middlesbrough stockbrokers, Todd and Crone, issued a statement that the 'London and provincial stock exchanges had closed until further orders owing to the war scare'. The Tees shipping trade was 'absolutely paralysed by the prevailing suspense' – many vessels were docked at Middlesbrough, uncertain as to their future movements. There was concern among local shipping firms about vessels at sea carrying cargoes that might be impounded in the case of war.

The effects of the 'scare' were felt in ordinary life too: housewives shopping in Linthorpe Road complained about the increase in food prices, despite local food retailers like Hinton's protesting that they were absorbing the rise.

August Bank Holiday, 1914

The fortnight's Territorial training coincided with the August bank holiday. On a day when many people traditionally took a trip to the countryside or to the seaside on one of the cheap North-Eastern Railway Company (NER) excursion trains, despite the crisis most events were advertised as still going ahead.

Saturday, 1 August
With the barometer rising, the forecast was favourable; the band of low pressure, which had brought the latest spell of poor weather, was moving across to Germany. The early trains leaving Middlesbrough were full of chattering day trippers, mothers laden with sandwiches, and children clutching their buckets and spades, all determined to make the most of the day. Bathers crowded onto the beaches on the Cleveland coast, the bathing machines in constant demand as people enjoyed the simple pleasure of the bracing sea air. The North Sea sparkled as the sun blazed down; men and women were paddling in the cold surf as they tried to avoid being splashed by their children. Occasionally a rumour would spread that a German battleship had been seen, and people giggled nervously at the thought that the Kaiser's navy could be somewhere just over the horizon.

In Redcar, they laughed and sang along with Sam Paul's Pierrots, dressed in their comical pantaloons costumes – Basil Hallam's 'Gilbert the Filbert' was a particular favourite with the audiences that summer. Elsewhere, crowds gathered on the esplanade where the melodious sounds of a brass band could be heard. At the Pier Pavilion, the 'Valentines' topped the bill. Two miles down the coast at Saltburn, Bert Grapho's Pierrots, now in their fifteenth summer at the resort, were entertaining a slightly less boisterous crowd. The Victorian Cliff Lift was busy all day, carrying people down to the beach, as it had done for thirty years. The Zetland Hotel, determined to make a special effort that weekend, was busy too, serving a 'superior luncheon' for its guests as they enjoyed glorious views of the fine golden sands and the sea beyond.

In Europe, the German government ordered a general mobilisation and declared war on Russia. With France mobilising too, many senior politicians thought that war was inevitable. In Britain, the Royal Navy was mobilised. Telegrams were sent out, and the police informed to deliver call-up papers. Wherever a crowd gathered to discuss the latest news, the question of hostilities was debated. As rumours multiplied it was becoming difficult to separate fact from hysteria. Political events took up a whole page in Saturday's *Sports Gazette*, much to the displeasure of local cricket fans, who wanted news of the North Yorkshire & South Durham cricket league.

A view down Albert Road of the Town Hall, the centre of civic life since it was opened in 1889. (Author's collection)

In the Town Hall at Middlesbrough, the Watch Committee assembled at 8 p.m. on Saturday evening. Town Council meetings on a Saturday evening were very unusual, a reflection of how serious the situation had become. Alderman Amos Hinton, in the chair, solemnly addressed colleagues to inform them that they must discuss the question of making suitable arrangements for efficiently 'policing the Borough' if a National Emergency arose in the next few days. The chief constable, Henry Riches, responded calmly, outlining arrangements already in place if such a contingency arose. Reassured, the council gave the chief constable plenary powers to meet any emergency that might arise, including extra policing if it was required. Although there were no troops on guard in Middlesbrough at this stage, it was reported in the local press that 'after a certain hour, constabulary are on duty at the Transporter Bridge'.

Sunday, 2 August
After Saturday's fine day there was heavy overnight rain, flooding some of the tents at the West Riding Territorials Training Camp in Marske and testing the usual good humour of the soldiers. The growing crisis forced NER to cancel all excursions. With all eyes on Europe, church services prayed for peace; although the Rev. Howard Hall, senior brigade chaplain at Marske, warned that despite the misery of war, there was one thing worse and that was a 'bastard peace, a peace at any price.' The sermons in most churches in Middlesbrough that Sunday morning also made reference to the possibility of war, voicing strong support for Great Britain to remain outside any conflict. There were two cabinet meetings that day, resulting in a policy decision to guarantee naval protection of French coasts against German aggression. When the cabinet was informed, during their second meeting, that the Germans had invaded Luxembourg, a sense of uneasiness was felt among those seated around the table.

Monday, 3 August
The weather on bank holiday Monday, 3 August 1914, turned out fine after a cloudy start. Despite the cancellation of all excursion

trains it was estimated that over 10,000 people arrived in Redcar by train that day. Saltburn also welcomed large crowds.

Following a decision made by the cabinet on Sunday afternoon to cancel Territorial training, the departure of over 3,000 Territorials for home, along with the call-up of navy reservists, placed a great strain on the resources of the railway companies. There wasn't enough rolling stock at Saltburn to take the troops back to the West Riding, so special trains were sent from Darlington and given precedence over all other traffic. Large crowds watched the arrival of the soldiers at Saltburn Station, cheering the trains as they departed and all along the route. Local retailers were not too pleased, as they had brought enough stock to supply the camp for a fortnight, and they were now left with lots of perishable unused stock. This forced them to head for the day trippers at the coast to salvage some lost sales.

Worried by the thoughts of a possible war many people remained at home, heading for Albert Park which, by the afternoon, was crowded with many young people having fun, oblivious to the grave situation and the worried looks on the faces of parents.

Although many of Middlesbrough's business leaders were away over the holiday weekend, those left behind were genuinely concerned about the prospect of war. One said he had over £20,000 worth of cargoes at sea which could be captured at any time. Another, echoing the views of Walter Cunliffe, Governor of the Bank of England, said a war involving England would be a major economic blunder.

On bank holiday Monday afternoon, Middlesbrough Station was very busy as reservists of one kind or another answered their call-up. Trains to Stockton overflowed with men from the Fleet Reserve and the Royal Naval Reserve travelling to catch a special train to Chatham. Amidst the enthusiastic send-off from relatives, one young naval reservist, having lost both legs in an accident, was wheeled onto the platform in a bath chair. Having received his papers like the others, he joined his companions in a rendition of their favourite songs. When he was wheeled up to a compartment door to shake hands with a fellow reservist boarding the train, he was heard to plead 'couldn't they just take me as a Marconi operator or something?' Adding to the noise and chaos of departing trains at Middlesbrough and Stockton there were many arrivals too, as the Territorials from Yorkshire and Durham returned from their training camps in Deganwy and Conway, North Wales.

Whilst these busy scenes were being repeated across the country, Edward Grey, looking 'pale, haggard and worn', addressed a full House of Commons at 3 p.m., updating them on the government's course of action and the motives behind it. The House applauded the decision not to commit the country to armed intervention as a response to the position in Serbia. Approval was given to the conditional promise of help from the navy regarding France, and the decision to help maintain the neutrality of Belgium. Following an adjournment, Grey again spoke to the House at 7 p.m., informing them that the German government had written to the Belgian government requesting free right of passage across Belgium for its troops if 'the necessity arose'. With Belgium's perpetual neutrality guaranteed by the European powers, including Germany, under the terms of the Treaty of London, signed in 1839, the Belgian King Albert I and his government declared their resolve to remain neutral and 'repel aggression by all possible means'.

Weary day trippers travelling home on Monday evening read in the *North-Eastern Daily Gazette* that with German troops having crossed the French frontier, the two countries were now at war. In London, as the lamps were being lit, Sir Edward Grey said 'the lamps are going out all over Europe; we shall not see them lit again in our lifetime'. Ominously, two or three war vessels, presumed to be British, were sighted off the Tees Bay later that same evening.

Tuesday, 4 August
When people awoke on Tuesday, 4 August 1914, the question, 'Will Britain go to war for France?' had been replaced by a new concern, 'Will Britain rescue Belgium?' There was a wave of support throughout Britain for 'poor little Belgium' and many felt Britain was under a moral obligation to offer them protection.

THE TERRITORIALS

The Territorial Army had been restructured in 1908.

One of the regular events was the annual camp, and 7,000 Territorials from Yorkshire and Durham had reached Deganwy and Conway on Sunday, 26 July 1914, for their annual training camp. In East Cleveland, 3,000 men of the West Riding Territorials arrived in pouring rain at Marske Station, from where they marched to their camp at Tofts Farm to begin their fifteen day stay. A YMCA tent was erected in each camp, and nightly concerts were arranged, featuring local artistes. Local officials from Redcar even visited to ensure that appropriate sanitation arrangements were in place. Training was well organised, and attracted a great deal of local attention.

The reservists' morale was boosted when news arrived on 30 July 1914 that the North Riding Territorial Association had decided that the Drill Hall in Abingdon Road, Middlesbrough, used by the 4th Battalion Yorkshire Regiment, would be upgraded. All companies of the national reserve raised in Middlesbrough would henceforth be known as the 'Middlesbrough Battalion North Riding Reserve'.

One of the more memorable visits to the training camps on the Cleveland coast was that of General French in 1908.

Souvenir of Gen: French's Visit to...

ON PARADE

HIGH ST. REDCAR

CHURCH SERVICE

GENERAL FRENCH.

REDCAR CAMP. 1908.

INSPECTING THE LINES

(Author's collection)

Germany had sent troops into Belgium early on 4 August, leading to a formal appeal from King Albert I to Britain for help. In Berlin, the British Ambassador presented Britain's ultimatum to Germany, requiring them to withdraw their troops from Belgium by midnight or 'she might consider herself to be at war with Great Britain'.

The uncertainty was making itself felt on the streets of Middlesbrough, with continued increases in the cost of food. The heavy demand for food, fuelled by panic buying over the weekend, continued on Tuesday with shops like the Co-operative Stores crowded with customers all day. A rush of people buying flour over the weekend was causing a shortage, as dealers couldn't renew their stocks. Some shops even closed for part of the day as they were behind in packing Saturday's orders, or they had suddenly found themselves short-staffed due to employees having been called up. Prices varied from hour to hour, with the price of flour reaching 2s 6d (12.5p) a stone, almost double what it was a week ago. Bread had gone up by ½d as bakers found it more difficult to obtain ingredients and with most of the sugar consumed in England at this time coming from Germany, unsurprisingly the price of sugar was high.

Middlesbrough Station was again full of Territorials and reservists having received their papers and leaving to answer their call-up (including several from Middlesbrough police force). Also passing through the station were groups of Germans off to join their regiments in Germany. The Netherlands Vice Consul at Middlesbrough, Mr C.A. Jervelund, asked any Dutch military personnel to return home, and if they had no means of travel they were advised to apply to the consulate in Zetland Road.

Even before the official full mobilisation of the British Army at 4 p.m. there were enthusiastic scenes in Middlesbrough. Rumours were at a fever pitch; someone said war had already been declared, someone else heard of a distressed vessel, which had been shelled, arriving at Middlesbrough Docks. It was alleged that an aeroplane or airship had flown down Linthorpe Road with a light attached.

Two Middlesbrough companies of 250 men from the 4th Battalion Alexandra's Own Territorial Regiment, having just arrived home on Monday evening from their camp in Wales, were hurriedly summoned to the Drill Hall on Tuesday morning. The order was so urgent that motor vehicles were sent to transport those who lived in outlying districts, whilst others simply had to leave their place of work. Once at the Drill Hall the men underwent a medical, and had expected to leave by noon. From 10 a.m. it was reported that hundreds of people were waiting outside expecting to cheer them off. As the hours passed the crowds got larger and finally, when the expected order had not been received by 9 p.m., Captain Bowes-Wilson, commanding the detachment, addressed the men amid 'remarkable scenes of enthusiasm' and dismissed them, with the order to reassemble at 7.30 a.m. the following morning!

In 1914, Thomas Duncan Henlock Stubbs, a 42-year-old Middlesbrough solicitor, a partner in the firm of Lucas, Hutchinson and Meek, lived comfortably with his family in Nunthorpe, which was then a small country hamlet south of Middlesbrough. His war diary records that, when he was out walking his dogs towards Nunthorpe Station at 7.15 p.m. on

Duncan Stubbs, a Middlesbrough solicitor, kept a diary of his experiences at the start of the war, the first page of which (Tuesday, 4 August 1914) is shown here in the background. (Courtesy of Alice Barrigan)

Tuesday evening, he saw a railway porter approaching with 'a telegram in his hand'. The two words it contained, 'Mobilise Adjutant' threw him into immediate action. As a captain in the Territorial Army in the Northumbrian (Heavy) Battery, Royal Garrison Artillery, he had expected to be called up immediately. Within an hour he was at the Drill Hall in Middlesbrough helping with the preparations for war. He returned home, just after the declaration of war at 11 p.m., to make his own arrangements to leave the following day. The future was uncertain but, like many others, he expected to be home soon.

In Middlesbrough it was an uneasy night, with a mood of subdued excitement – an inescapable acknowledgment that Britain would soon be at war. The general feeling was that this critical state of affairs had arisen very suddenly and, for many people, the past ten days had been an emotional roller coaster, encompassing feelings ranging from depression to excitement. Now, with the Foreign Office confirming that from 11 p.m. on 4 August a state of war existed between the two countries, the tension ended, the waiting was over, replaced by the powerful compulsion to do the 'honourable thing and rise to the challenge'.

2

'WE DON'T WANT TO LOSE YOU'

First Day of War

In a modern day world of twenty-four hour news, imagine the position of those who lived in Middlesbrough in 1914 – dependent on newspapers, rumour and speculation to sustain any intelligence of world events. This helps to explain why the First World War was able to develop almost unnoticed. There was no desire for war in Middlesbrough, but people quickly rallied to the cause. The role of Britain as protector of Belgium appealed, and created an astonishing collective enthusiasm. Literally over-night, great excitement, albeit tinged with apprehension, fear and panic, became the mood of the day.

This was to be a very different experience of war. The psycho-logical need to come to terms with an unfamiliar situation by cross-referencing it against experiential history was a struggle for most people. Though most still remembered the South African War in 1899, and some the war in Crimea in 1855, these were distant conflicts with a limited impact on daily life in Britain. With invasion considered a possibility, this war would touch everyone. The universal public aim to win the war would sweep all before it, yet privately individuals struggled to adjust. To support them there was a need for government, as well as civic, leadership at a local level. To expedite both required the voluntary commitment of the people as a whole.

DORA (Defence of the Realm Act) was regularly updated, with the government constantly giving itself new powers and introducing new restrictions on everything from using petrol to turning on the lights, a ban on flying kites and feeding bread to animals. The best-known example of DORA is probably the introduction of British Summer Time in 1916.

The government exercised close control of everyday life through the Defence of the Realm Act (DORA), passed on 8 August only four days after war began. DORA had an immediate impact on the lives of most people. The local authorities were the conduit for the day-to-day enforcement of these powers.

The war was everywhere you turned, whether you were a housewife shopping in Linthorpe Road or a riverside worker made unemployed. The *North-Eastern Daily Gazette*, despite censorship, rhetorical bias and propaganda, tried to give an overview of events. An extensive listing of those 'called to the colours' and full details of the British and German Fleets in the North Sea was printed, including the date of commission, size and name of the officer in charge of each ship. Just to ensure the public knew who was fighting whom, a list of 'The Belligerents' was printed showing the enemies and allies of each country.

The launch of Kitchener's 'Call to Arms' campaign was heavily publicised in local newspapers using full page advertisements like this. (Courtesy of the Evening Gazette, *Middlesbrough)*

Across the country the railway system was stretched to its limits. Thousands of men bound for the army left their homes, either as part of the British Expeditionary Force *en route* to France, or travelling to a regimental training camp.

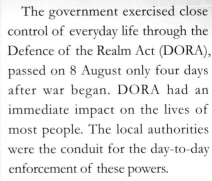

Your King and Country Need You.

A CALL TO ARMS.

An addition of 100,000 men to His Majesty's Regular Army is immediately necessary in the present grave national emergency.

Lord Kitchener is confident that this appeal will be at once responded to by all those who have the safety of our Empire at heart.

TERMS OF SERVICE.

General Service for a period of 3 years or until the war is concluded.

Age of enlistment between 19 and 30.

HOW TO JOIN.

Full information can be obtained at any Post Office in the Kingdom, or at any Military Depot.

God Save the King.

Off You Go Then, Lads

It was estimated that over 1,000 men left Middlesbrough during that first day. Many, like Thomas Duncan Henlock Stubbs ('Duncan' or 'TDH' to his family), had been leading ordinary lives only a few days before. His words capture the atmosphere of that day. Following the proclamations of war on Tuesday night, Stubbs wrote in his diary that he had risen early on Wednesday morning and caught the 5.30 a.m. train to Middlesbrough. He arrived at the Drill Hall to find everyone already extremely busy, as the Middlesbrough Battery of the Northumberland Royal Garrison Artillery was on parade at 6 a.m. Stubbs joined a line of men awaiting their medical. When Doctor Longbotham placed his stethoscope over Stubbs' chest he said, 'I don't care whether you pass me

> Major Thomas Duncan Henlock Stubbs ('Duncan') served at the Western Front 1915–17, then served at Aldershot until 1919, when he came home. He died in 1931.

or not I am going so you need not trouble'. The first forty men who were passed fit went off to Monkseaton, the artillery's training camp, to collect horses and wagons. The next twelve went off to Redcar to collect 192 rounds of ammunition.

Throughout the morning there were telegraph and telephone messages, and preparations were made for their departure, loading up the armaments train at Middlesbrough Station with guns and horses, newly purchased by Colonel Douglas. There were a 'hundred and one things necessary' including sharpening the swords of the officers until Stubbs 'could almost shave with it'. Stubbs went on his motorcycle to the National Provincial Bank to collect £1,300, enough to pay each man his bounty of £5 5s (£5.25) for enlisting. Although the banks had been closed since the previous week, Mr Eltenton, the manager, ensured that the cheque was cashed. Captain Winterschladen lent Stubbs his car to travel back to the Drill Hall, and at 10 a.m. Stubbs records that, 'being famished', he went to take breakfast at his club, the Cleveland Club in Exchange Place, where he also took the chance to say goodbye to many of his friends.

After his busy morning, Stubbs returned home at 1 p.m. on his motorcycle to get his belongings and say goodbye to his 38-year-old wife, Madge, his son Hugh, aged 13, and his 9-year-old daughter, Katherine (who burst into tears), before catching the 1.37 p.m. train back to Middlesbrough. Although calm himself, he notes that his wife was 'feeling the occasion' – particularly as their 15-year-old son, John Duncan, a naval cadet, had been called up to HMS *Aboukir*. Sadly, only forty-eight days later the *Aboukir* was an early victim of the war, being sunk along with HMS *Hogue* and HMS *Cressy* in the North Sea by a U-boat, early one morning on 22 September 1914. Stubbs, stationed at Monkseaton, received a short telegram from the Admiralty, saying: 'Regret to inform you that your son is not amongst those saved.'

Back in Middlesbrough, after leaving his family, Stubbs looked in again at his club where he saw his father and several friends, many of whom wished they themselves were going off to war. By late afternoon the Northumberland Royal Garrison Artillery was finally ready to depart, and with over 100 men leaving this was a momentous event. The constant sound of patriotic songs filled the air, as the band of the local National Reserve and the crowd gave the soldiers a musical accompaniment as they marched smartly down Albert Road to the station. The streets around Middlesbrough Station were filled with people cheering. Stubbs walked through the crowd, later writing that he 'had laid in some provisions and most fortunate it was that I did so'.

So many crowds filled the streets that the station gates had to be closed to the public, with only friends of the officers and men being allowed into the station and onto the platform. Among the large crowd gathered to see them depart was Stubbs' father, as well as his former OC (Officer Commanding), Penry Williams, the mayor and mayoress and Chief Constable Henry Riches.

The troop train steamed in, pulling a heavy load of armaments: 'four heavy cannon, six ammunition wagons, forty-five horses & the carriages for officers & men'. Boarding their train the soldiers, dressed in full khaki, appeared brave, their faces set with determination. The atmosphere was charged with intense emotion. The strains of 'Auld Lang Syne' and 'God Save the King' could be heard and the noise of carriage doors being slammed shut echoed around the station roof. As the guard blew his whistle, a blast of steam from the engine instigated a succession of final hugs and kisses. There came a high-pitched screech as the engine wheels spun round with the strain of pulling such a large load. The world seemed to stop for a moment, before the train moved slowly away from the platform. Amidst cheering and waving of handkerchiefs, shouts of 'goodbye and good luck!' filled the air, until the khaki-clad arms of the men waving from the train could be seen no more.

For those on the train it was to be a remarkable journey. Stubbs records that, as the train passed the Linthorpe Road railway crossing, he 'looked out and saw the whole street simply packed with cheering people [and] it was the same all along the route, at every village and home, people were cheering and waving as we passed'.

An hour later, at 5 p.m., it was the turn of the Middlesbrough Company of the Royal Engineers to depart from the station.

These poignant scenes were played out at railway stations throughout the region. At Stokesley, the Territorials, having just returned from North Wales on Monday, 3 August 1914, were mobilised on the Tuesday, and left for their war base on the train on Wednesday. In a memorable send-off, with cheers from the large crowd, the Hartlepool Operatic Band marched with the men along the High Street to Stokesley Station. Eyewitnesses said 'every eye was wet, as the hymn "God be with you till we meet again" was sung, before the khaki-clad defenders of the country' were on their way.

Men, Men and More Men

People supported the war in different ways. By mid-August 300 reservists were drilling three times a week at the Hugh Bell Schools after the mayor had arranged for the playgrounds at the Middlesbrough High School and Hugh Bell Schools to be used. Families in Middlesbrough took pride in sending someone off to fight for king and country, many displaying a notice in their window to that effect. When Laurence F. Gjers was appointed to command the Middlesbrough Battalion, North Riding of Yorkshire National Reserve, he contributed a full set of ambulance stretchers and dressings.

The organising officer of the Middlesbrough Battalion of the National Reserve, Major G. Rance, made an appeal on 10 August 1914 for all men under the age of 55 who had served in the army or navy to come forward and register for service. There was an immediate response and over 400 men reported at the National Reserve headquarters at 53 Grange Road West in the

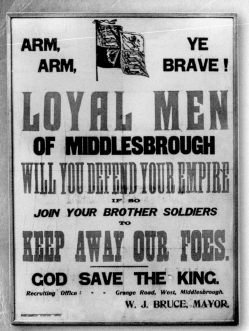

ARM, ARM, **YE BRAVE !**

LOYAL MEN OF MIDDLESBROUGH

WILL YOU DEFEND YOUR EMPIRE

IF SO

JOIN YOUR BROTHER SOLDIERS

TO

KEEP AWAY OUR FOES.

GOD SAVE THE KING.

Recruiting Office : - - Grange Road, West, Middlesbrough.

W. J. BRUCE, MAYOR.

This poster accompanied Mayor W.J. Bruce's emotive appeal for men to enlist in August 1914. (Courtesy of Teesside Archives)

first twenty-four hours, resulting in the recruiting officers running out of forms. The following day, the Middlesbrough recruiting office was literally besieged, and on several occasions the door had to be locked against those waiting outside.

Men who enlisted received huge public support – the boy next door or gent who lived down the street became overnight heroes. Large crowds gathered to watch the men go into the recruiting office, cheering and clapping them as they did so.

They won the hearts of fellow citizens in other ways too. Thomas Burdon, the licensee of the Albert Park Hotel, Middlesbrough, in court for reckless driving at Hartburn, was only charged with 'costs' when he claimed he was only speeding because, having just been called up, he was in a hurry to do his duty. Another man charged with speeding, Thomas Stark, said in his defence that having joined the Royal Flying Corps, he was rushing around saying goodbye to relatives. Although Chief Constable Henry Riches was a hardened police officer, he decided in the circumstances not to charge Stark. Another man charged with theft asked if he could be excused the sentence he had been given if he joined up; he duly enlisted the next day.

The new Secretary for War, Lord Kitchener, immediately asked for 100,000 new recruits. Civic leaders throughout the land were urged to get the people to understand the gravity of the situation. In Middlesbrough, the mayor wrote an open letter to the *North-Eastern Daily Gazette* asking for volunteers, and issued his own appeal:

> Arm! Arm, ye brave! Loyal men of Middlesbrough will you defend your Empire? If so, join your brother soldiers to keep away our foes.

With this intense pressure it is not surprising perhaps that the national target was achieved in just two weeks. This 'First Kitchener's New Army', which included many men from Middlesbrough, was known as 'K1'. A call for another 100,000 men to form K2 was made on 28 August 1914. This target was also met in a very short time, with the result that the *North-Eastern Daily Gazette* reported on 3 September that a 'Third New Army' of 100,000 men was now being called for.

Recruitment on a Street Corner

Although men were signing up at Middlesbrough, there was the feeling that it could be better. The *North-Eastern Daily Gazette* reported, on 27 August 1914, that while many Teesside men had already volunteered for military service, many had still to answer the call. In the week beginning Monday, 24 August 1914, for example, the numbers enlisting were: Monday 100, Tuesday 129 and eighty-four on Wednesday – respectable totals, but mainly men with some sort of military experience, who walked in from the street to join up. To increase numbers, it was necessary to attract those who had never served before, especially young men.

There were issues to sort out, however. Many local young men were concerned about leaving their jobs and therefore more firms had to be encouraged to support volunteers by holding open their jobs. Then there were the substantial delays at the recruiting office; a lack of clerical staff meant that the formalities of joining up – the paperwork, medical, the swearing in by a magistrate – took longer to process, leading to queues of men outside the office for much of the day.

The news from Belgium and France was worrying; besieged Namur had fallen and the medieval town of Louvain had suffered heavy damage. The front pages of the newspapers were filled with details of the British Expeditionary Force's first major action and subsequent retreat at Mons. When it emerged, in late August, that the Germans were so close to Paris that the French government had been forced to move to Bordeaux, the need for more volunteers to come forward became critical. Clearly a well-organised, coordinated recruitment drive was necessary if the flow of recruits was to increase sufficiently.

On the evening of Thursday, 27 August 1914, Alderman Alfred Mattison organised a public meeting in the Committee Room of the Town Hall, inviting 'all persons willing to interest themselves in assisting Recruiting' to attend. Presided over by the mayor, the aim was to help in 'formulating a Scheme to assist Recruiting in this District'. The *North-Eastern Daily Gazette* set the mood for the evening:

> Already Teesside has sent many of her sons to fight their country's battle, but there remain many young men who have hitherto turned a deaf ear to the call for service. Maybe they have not yet realised the urgency of the need, but they will not long remain in ignorance.

Following a number of full-blooded speeches urging the need to take action now, a Recruitment Committee was formed. This was a turning point in recruitment in 1914. Before the compulsory nature of the Derby Scheme in 1915 and the 1916 Military Service Act, the Recruitment Committee played an important role in promoting recruitment in Middlesbrough, being particularly successful during the early months of the war when a record number of recruits signed up for service. Its chief role would be to oversee, what Mattison called, 'a sustained recruitment drive throughout the whole of the Middlesbrough area'. This 'rally to the colours' would be induced through a series of strictly 'no politics' meetings, a platform for speakers whose only aim was to raise men for the military forces.

Nine men attended the inaugural meeting of the Recruitment Committee at 3 p.m. on Friday, 28 August 1914, chaired by the mayor, Alderman W.J. Bruce. A list of thirty-three speakers was compiled, and eleven car owners came forward to answer an appeal to help with transport. One of the committee's first tasks was to finalise arrangements for the open-air meeting taking place later that day. The meeting, which claimed to be one of the first of its kind anywhere in the country, was held at the Infirmary Corner, off Newport Road, at 7.30 p.m.

The evening began with a procession from the railway station, headed by a group of Boy Scouts, followed by motor vehicles and a large crowd, with a band playing 'patriotic airs' all along the route. Approaching Infirmary Corner they were met by a large noisy gathering waiting to cheer them on. Copies of the *Gazette*'s list of all those 'brave men', who had already enlisted, were freely handed around.

Prominent members of local political parties put aside their differences to unite for the evening. The speakers, Alderman Alfred Mattison, Captain Bunn, Councillors Turner and Emanuel Spence and Mr H. Sugden, all received rapturous applause as they addressed the meeting in the fading evening light. Councillor Spence received a particularly huge cheer from the crowd, after his attempt to form a local civic guard two weeks earlier. Infused with patriotic fervour the boisterous meeting concluded with the national anthem 'rendered with great gusto by a tremendous crowd … before a rush of young men all eager to register themselves in their country's cause' went to sign on in the Infirmary's outpatient department, converted to a recruiting office for the evening. A huge response of over 200 men came forward to enlist. The event, an enormous success, was described as being the 'largest and most enthusiastic open-air meeting for many a long day in Middlesbrough'. The enthusiasm continued over the weekend, as a 'healthy and reassuring wave of patriotism … [swept] over the Middlesbrough district'.

Two more meetings, billed as 'The War and the Needs of a Nation', took place on Sunday, 30 August. A crowd of several thousand assembled in Albert Park at 3.15 p.m., around a flag-bedecked platform where a group of speakers, including Penry Williams, once again addressed the crowd with the Erimus Silver Band playing well-known patriotic songs. Afterwards, the recruitment committee was virtually besieged by men coming forward.

A MEETING
To-Night, Friday,
AT
Infirmary Corner, Newport Road,
7-30 p.m
THE WAR AND THE NEEDS OF THE NATION.
SPEAKERS :
**Alderman A. Mattison,
Captain Bunn,
Alderman Poole,
Councillor Turner,
Councillor Emanuel Spence,
Mr. H. Sugden.**
Rally Round the Old Flag!
Jordison & Co., Ld., Printers, Middlesbrough.

A poster for what is believed to be the first open-air recruitment meeting to be held in the country, on Infirmary Corner, Friday, 28 August 1914. (Courtesy of Teesside Archives)

There were more, fervent scenes at the other meeting held later that day at 8 p.m. in Middlesbrough Market Place. Young men who registered with the officers were told to report at the recruiting office in Middlesbrough – addresses of local recruiting offices were printed in the *North-Eastern Daily Gazette*.

The introduction of the Recruitment Committee had an immediate effect, with almost 1,000 names put forward in the last few days of August, a marked increase in those joining up. To resolve the complaints received about queuing from men joining up earlier, another recruiting office was opened in Middlesbrough, at the Dunning Street entrance to the Town Hall. Facilities at Grange Road West were extended too, when the adjacent house became part of the recruitment offices. It wasn't possible to please everyone, however; the displaced tenant from the house ended up being arrested and fined in court after having gone in a drunken state to the Drill Hall to lodge his objections to the plan.

Middlesbrough, like the country as a whole, experienced record levels of recruitment at the beginning of September 1914. Much of this local increase was due to the success of the open-air meetings. The Recruitment Committee's list of planned meetings for the period Sunday, 30 August, to Friday, 4 September, illustrate the intensity of their campaign. Following the busy weekend already described, Alderman T.G. Poole led another open-air meeting at 7.30 p.m. on Monday, 31 August, at the corner of Borough Road West and Linthorpe Road, after which a record 465 men enlisted. On Tuesday there were two meetings scheduled, 12.15 p.m. at Bell Bros. Ironworks at Port Clarence, and 7.30 p.m. at Stockton Street Recreation Ground. Wednesday was similar, with meetings taking place simultaneously at 7.30 p.m. in North Ormesby Market Place and at Grand Hotel Corner in Zetland Road. When 474 enlisted the following day, there were hopes of reaching 2,000 recruits in a week.

Having put their names forward, the men came to the recruitment office to complete the formalities. Long queues formed outside the Town Hall and Grange Road West, before the recruitment offices opened at 9 a.m. Men stood for so long that food had to be organised for them. Despite the offices being open from 9.30 a.m. to 8 p.m., some clerks had to work to 11 p.m. in order to deal with the paperwork. Exasperated the mayor, Alderman Bruce, sent a telegram to Lord Kitchener on 1 September informing him, in brief but precise terms, that:

> Hundreds of men wishing to join. Cannot do so on account of lack of clerical labour required to attest a man. If the form was simplified to just six questions with a place for officials to sign, then Middlesbrough could send thousands instead of hundreds … wire instructions immediately.

The War Office, anxious for men, forwarded the telegram to Captain Morris Moore, the chief commander at York, and five clerks from local businesses were brought in to help out.

A CALL ❧ TO ARMS

In connection with Miss GERTRUDE BELL'S Lecture :

'OUR DEBT TO BELGIUM'

To be given in the ARTHUR HEAD SCHOOL, on

THURSDAY EVENING, OCTOBER 29TH, 1914

A

RECRUITING PARADE

WILL BE HELD IN THORNABY

THE NATIONAL RESERVE (THORNABY COMPANY)
1ST THORNABY (VIC.) TROOP BOY SCOUTS

Accompanied by their Brass Band

will Parade at the FIVE LAMPS at 7-15 p.m. and proceed by way of George Street, Francis Street, Gilmour Street, Thornaby Road, George Street, New Street, Mandale Road, Swarthmore Terrace and Mansfield Street to the

🇬🇧 ARTHUR HEAD SCHOOL 🇬🇧

in time for the Lecture at 8-0 p.m. The Scouts will distribute leaflets en route.

At the conclusion of the Lecture

MAJOR G. RANCE, C.R.O., Middlesbrough.
CAPT. J. O'SULLIVAN, R.O., Thornaby.
CAPT. H. BUNN, Eaglescliffe.

will speak (by kind permission of the Mayor and the Lecturer).

In the present grave National Emergency all Thornaby men eligible for enlistment are invited to attend this Lecture.

FOR KING AND COUNTRY.
GOD SAVE THE KING !

Gertrude Bell did a lot of speaking at recruitment meetings, and this poster is from one of the many venues she appeared at in the autumn of 1914, before she went off to work with the British Red Cross in France, in November 1914. (Courtesy of Teesside Archives)

Some of the biggest audiences were at meetings that featured well-known respected public figures. One such occasion was the visit of Gertrude Bell to the Town Hall in Middlesbrough on Thursday, 3 September. Gertrude Bell had a strong local connection, being the daughter of Sir Hugh Bell, a highly regarded local iron-master living at Rounton Grange, south of Yarm. Interestingly, Bell made it known prior to the meeting that she preferred that her meetings 'should not appear to be called and supported by the Recruiting Authorities, [although] she would not object to Officers recruiting among the audience when she had finished speaking'.

Bell really enthused the large crowd with her eloquent oratory, as she addressed the audience with her rousing theme 'Why England is at War?' Recalling the sequence of events following the assassination of Archduke Ferdinand of Austria, she shrewdly made it clear that this wasn't the reason for Britain's entry into the war. 'Consider the bargain that Germany had offered to Britain before she marched into Belgium – wasn't the war being fought in the cause of civilisation and democracy?' Bell knew how to keep the interest of the crowd to the end by finishing with an emotional personal reference to the Yorkshire Regiment, in which her brother served. Everyone got to their feet, cheering as they did so. The tumultuous applause was still going on as Alderman Alfred Mattison and Councillor Spence thanked Bell, and the national anthem was being sung. On the next day, Friday, 4 September 1914, for the fourth consecutive day, a new record was established with 550 men joining up, 400 of them at the Town Hall – forcing the original target for the week of 2,000 men to be revised upwards to 3,000.

The Friday evening open-air meeting held at the corner of East Street and Cleveland Street in the old town, was a very feisty gathering as a number of very spirited and experienced speakers, including Penry Williams, challenged the audience to 'rally round the old flag'. The evening was another huge success, however, with 837 men enlisting the next day as Saturday, 5 September, established another new record for recruitment on a single day. Furthermore, the weekly total of 3,237 recruits was also a record.

On Sunday, 6 September, the *North-Eastern Daily Gazette* published a 'War Special Edition'. The two page special featured details of the brave and glorious British retreat back to south of the Marne, along with a full page war map. However, the newspaper's patriotic rhetoric couldn't mask the depressing news that 15,000 casualties had been reported from the past ten days of fighting. Publishing a Sunday edition was not without its problems. Complaints were made about newspaper boys shouting too loud and making too much noise for a Sunday evening. Instructions were issued, forbidding shouting after 6.30 p.m. and the sale of papers near to a church, or during the times when there was a church service.

Later that evening, Martin Harvey, appearing that week at the Grand Opera House, delivered a lecture there on 'The War'. A well-known actor and dramatist, Harvey had just returned from a successful tour of America, and had been asked to do the lecture tour by the prime minister, Herbert Asquith. The mayor opened the evening by thanking Harvey for choosing Middlesbrough as his first venue. As he walked on stage to address the large crowd, Harvey won the audience over from the start:

> My dear fellow Britons, if ever a Briton had reason to be proud that he was a citizen of the Empire it was today. If you are among the lucky ones you will be sent out to the front line [where] British soldiers are always to be found, just as they were at Mons the other day [applause], when the Kaiser threw the pick of his troops at them and then failed to break the line [wild applause and cheers].

After the meeting, a collection raised £19 10s (£19.50) for the Prince of Wales National Relief Fund.

Not all meetings were this theatrical. J. Foster Fraser, chairman of the London War Society was praised for his prosaic and informative lecture, at the Grand Opera House on 27 September 1914, on the virtue of the war, which was illustrated by slides lent by the press agencies. Sir Arthur Conan Doyle addressed a large crowd at the Town Hall on 13 March 1915, on 'The Great Battles of the

War', talking about the battles so far and explaining why Britain had to win. The well-known orator, Horatio Bottomley, with his own unique view of the war, attracted a huge crowd when he appeared at Middlesbrough Town Hall on 12 October 1915. Bottomley's jingoistic rhetoric gained a standing ovation from the audience, reflecting the town's nationalistic mood.

Other distinguished figures visiting Middlesbrough included the chief Scout, General Sir Robert Baden-Powell, who spoke to an audience of over 3,000 people at Middlesbrough Town Hall on 1 November 1916. Baden-Powell talked of the heroism of the military, including Jack Cornwell, a shining example to all young Scouts in the audience. The Home Secretary, Sir George Cave, accompanied by his predecessor, Sir Herbert Samuel, spoke to a capacity audience at Middlesbrough Town Hall on 18 January 1917, about the new 'War Loan' being introduced by the government.

However, the most distinguished visitors to Middlesbrough during the war were almost certainly King George V and Queen Mary, who came on 13 June 1917 to 'inspect and encourage the work that was being done in the Munitions Works, Docks and Shipyards'.

Penry Williams was the Liberal MP for Middlesbrough from 1910. He took an active part in town life, particularly the recruitment campaign of 1914, before he enlisted with one of the pioneer units in Gloucestershire. (Courtesy of Middlesbrough Reference Library)

Your King Wants You !   Your Country Wants You !

Your Chums Want You !   I Want You !

COLONEL PENRY WILLIAMS,
Commanding the 4th Yorks. (2nd line).

With the number of volunteers totalling almost 5,000 there was a shortage of uniforms for the new recruits, and Major Rance announced that 10s (50p) would be paid to any new recruit who produced, in serviceable condition, a great coat, boots and suit, until a uniform could be issued. So many men volunteered in Middlesbrough during this record-breaking week that recruitment was suspended for a week from Monday, 7 September 1914, until the clerical congestion was sorted out. When recruitment began again some of the impetus had been lost, possibly as a result of changes from the War Office to ease the congestion. The increase in the minimum height and chest measurement immediately reduced numbers and only sixty-one signed up on the first day. The downward trend in recruitment figures continued, much to the alarm of the local and national authorities, forcing a reduction of the minimum height and an increase in the age limit to 38. The numbers increased again after the First Battle of Ypres in November 1914, but this was short-lived.

Specific groups of men who were believed not to be 'doing their duty' were targeted, including businessmen and the youth of the town. At one public rally the mayor spoke of seeing 'hundreds of youths leaving the football game at Ayresome Park the previous evening seemingly indifferent to the war'. He made a direct challenge to the young men in the audience: 'The sons of Town Councillors have enlisted – who of you would now come forward?' Despite over 100 men doing so, the young men of Middlesbrough again came in for criticism from the mayor when he commented at a meeting that they should join up immediately, or face 'a white feather distribution if the call went unheeded'. This was deemed self-contradictory, especially as he had just praised Middlesbrough for supplying twice its pro rata quota of recruits for a town of its population size.

Recruitment meetings were not just held in the town. The prospect of a captive audience made local works and factories a popular location for recruitment meetings. Speakers were keen to attend these gatherings, with patriotic feelings easily aroused among workers. Over 2,000 men attended one such meeting at Bolckow Vaughan and Co. Cleveland Iron and Steel Works.

So successful was the recruitment committee at Middlesbrough that Preston Kitchen, the town clerk, sent letters to other local towns, offering to arrange for speakers to come to meetings in their town should they care to arrange one. A group of speakers, including Gertrude Bell and Colonel W.H.A. Wharton of Skelton Castle, travelled to open-air meetings throughout the region.

Admiral Charles Fitzgerald started the 'White Feather Movement' in August 1914. It encouraged young women to target and give out in public white feathers to young men eligible to sign up. These often indiscriminate actions caused much distress, especially where there was a legitimate reason for not enlisting.

One town taking up the offer was Redcar, where, after passionate speeches by Alderman Alfred Mattison, the crowds sang an emotional rendition of 'It's a long way to Tipperary'. Their well-rehearsed routine made the most of these highly charged affairs. Colonel Wharton opened the meeting by highlighting that the country was facing its greatest crisis, and that the young men who didn't come forward now would rue the day if the Germans triumphed. Gertrude Bell spoke for nearly an hour, giving a detailed explanation of the events leading up to the war, the moral outrage of invading a small country like Belgium and how terrible it would be for England if Germany were allowed to triumph. Bell made a special appeal to women to play their part by encouraging their 'menfolk' to volunteer. These meetings were effective – over twenty men joined up at Skinningrove, forty at Loftus and eight at Skelton – a high ratio considering the number of eligible men available.

Reports of atrocities in Belgium, and British Expeditionary Force casualties at Mons, were creating increasing unrest in the town. One evening, crowds of over 1,000 people, gathered at the station to watch a large batch of volunteer recruits depart, only to find they were barred from admittance. For a while they cheered and sang songs good-heartedly, before the mood changed and those near to the gates rushed the police. Having pushed back the sliding gates to gain admission to the station they were reported as giving their patriotism 'further whole-hearted expression'. It was mob-rule nevertheless. On another occasion there were more rousing scenes when enormous crowds gathered to watch a large number of recruits march to Middlesbrough Station to entrain. To avoid trouble, Middlesbrough Police and the Railway Police lined Albert Road, as the soldiers marched along singing 'We are Fred Karno's Army', watched by mothers, sisters and sweethearts, all weeping and waving.

Support for the recruitment campaign was widespread. Colonel Chaloner at Guisborough Hall reportedly told his agent that any men who volunteered for service were to have their cottages rent-free whilst they were away on service. Lord Furness also issued a similar statement to those who lived on his estates in Middlesbrough,

Darlington and West Hartlepool. In South Bank, Alexander Cross and Sons Ltd offered to pay a £5 bounty to the first fifty men who volunteered for Kitchener's Second Army. Many companies made firm commitments to any men who went off to war that their jobs would be waiting for them when they returned. J. Newhouse and Co. Ltd, drapers of Middlesbrough, went one step further beyond giving an assurance about jobs – they suggested that all male employees of eligible age should immediately volunteer for service.

On 15 September 1914 Middlesbrough Football Club announced, after receiving a request from the War Office, that 'they would give every facility and assistance to recruiting at our matches & also to any Speakers who may care to attend'. Ayresome Park was available for drilling, and the club also allowed Middlesbrough Miniature Rifle Club, to use their practice range at the ground in order to train men to use a rifle. Initially the sessions were held on three evenings a week, but these soon became

In the autumn of 1914 a lot of pressure was brought to bear on young men who had not already enlisted. This cartoon 'King or Football?' is aimed at the fact that League football continued during the first year of the war, whilst many thought it should be shut down. (Courtesy of the Evening Gazette, Middlesbrough)

available every weekday and all day Sunday, with one evening session for ladies. Middlesbrough FC players also received some military training, including instruction from Inspector Seymour of Middlesbrough Police on using the Lee Enfield rifle. A minute from a board meeting on 2 November 1914, states that, 'it was decided to purchase 2 leather jackets & a pair of Helmets for protection of Players during Fencing [sic] practice'.

The military authorities struggled to cope with the overwhelming numbers of volunteers. Town Clerk Preston Kitchen, wrote to Major Rance (recruiting officer for Middlesbrough) on 21 October 1914, to say that his office had been 'besieged by hundreds of women who had received no Separation Allowance since their husbands had joined up, in some cases two months previously'. Kitchen also noted complaints received about living conditions for recruits at their training depot, and the delay in being allotted a regimental number, which effectively meant they were not being paid. Having mentioned the reluctance of recruitment committee members to continue supporting Kitchener's latest appeal for 500,000 men with such matters unresolved, the mayor was able to report within a week that all matters had been resolved, and recruitment meetings could begin again.

Many local men enlisted with the 4th Yorkshire Regiment. At the request of the North Riding Territorial Association, Lt Col T. Gibson Poole VD opened a recruiting office at 131 Linthorpe Road, and installed himself as Honorary Recruiting Officer. Between 5 May 1915 and 12 January 1916 (when Poole moved on to a new post at Retford), he had enrolled 1,342 recruits out of a total of 2,000 men.

'C'mon the Boro Lads ...' the Teesside Battalion

Early in the war, when there was an undeniable *Boy's Own* spirit of adventure among recruits, the thought of going to war with your friends or workmates in a 'Pals' Battalion', as they became known, caught on very quickly. The idea is thought to have originated from

General Sir Henry Rawlinson's suggestion in August 1914 that men would be more likely to join up if they knew they were going to serve alongside friends or work colleagues. Local variations of this theme included the announcement, on 16 September, of the formation of a company of Middlesbrough High School old boys to be attached to H Company of the Reserve Battalion 4th Yorkshire Regiment being raised at Northallerton by Colonel Wharton.

The Teesside Battalion was officially raised in January 1915, and this recruiting poster is a part of their short-lived history. Note the training is to be at Marton Hall. (Courtesy of Teesside Archives)

Kitchener's Army

The new Secretary for War, Lord Kitchener, made it clear from the start that he envisaged this being a long war, and that the one resource that would be needed was men, men and more men. Regular army recruitment still existed, as did joining the Special Reserve and the Territorial Forces. Backed by authorisation from parliament, he launched a 'call to arms' on 11 August 1914, asking for 100,000 men to enlist for his 'New Army'. As an incitement to join up, Kitchener offered a new form of short service, which allowed a recruit to serve for either three years, or for the duration of the war, whichever was longest.

There began an extraordinary campaign of mass persuasion by the government. One of the chief weapons were posters and leaflets, which town councils could order free of charge from the Parliamentary Recruiting Committee. The posters appeared everywhere in Middlesbrough, including Alfred Leete's famous poster 'Lord Kitchener Wants You'. The iconic image of Kitchener pointing his finger quickly became part of the government's poster offensive after first appearing on 5 September 1914 as the cover of a popular magazine, *London Opinion*. The whole of society urged men to 'do their duty' and men continually faced the questions: 'Wouldn't they feel guilty if they did nothing?' 'Where was their masculine pride?' 'Didn't they fear invasion?'

The Teesside Battalion were based at Marton Hall for their training in the spring of 1915.

Marton Hall. (Courtesy of Teesside Archives)

Although not strictly a 'Pal's Battalion', by the end of 1914 a local company, the Teesside Battalion, was on the verge of being raised. The first recorded notion of the idea is in a letter, sent on 9 November 1914 to the mayor, Alderman Bruce, by Major William Fleming of Cornfield Road, Linthorpe. Fleming wanted to highlight the fact that a town like Middlesbrough, with its many advantages, including location and its large male population, did not have a single soldier stationed there. Continuing his theme, he felt that if a public-spirited man could raise a battalion called the Teesside, Middlesbrough or Cleveland Battalion, it would be a great success and seriously improve local recruitment. Fleming's ideas won immediate written support from the mayor. Always enthusiastic to demonstrate his leadership of the war effort in Middlesbrough, Bruce also wrote directly to Lord Kitchener requesting 'advice' on the raising of a local battalion using Fleming's ideas to support his case. Intriguingly, there is no acknowledgement of Fleming's role, nor is he mentioned in any subsequent newspaper reports regarding the new battalion.

The minutes of the Recruitment Committee, 23 November 1914, record that a letter had been received from the Secretary of the War Office 'stating that the Army Council would welcome the formation of a Middlesbrough Battalion'. Two names were proposed – Middlesbrough Battalion and the Teesside Battalion, the latter being preferred, as it offered a broader geographical appeal. Major Fleming was present to hear this news – though he was named as one of the accredited speakers on the committee's list compiled in August 1914, he didn't usually attend these meetings. The minutes of the meeting record that the only time Major Fleming spoke was to reiterate the contents of his original letter to the mayor.

The idea of a new battalion ran into local opposition. Waynman Dixon, director of Middlesbrough shipbuilders, Raylton, Dixon & Co. Ltd, wrote to the mayor to say that, being busy with Admiralty contracts and having already lost 25 per cent of their young efficient workers, any further loss might lead to orders being suspended and men being laid off. Moreover, having contributed many men already 'the attention of the

Recruiting Authorities should be directed more to Agricultural and rural districts'. A notice was even displayed at their shipyard making it quite clear that no worker would be allowed to enlist for the new battalion without special permission from the firm.

The mayor, Alderman W.J. Bruce, called a special Recruitment Committee meeting for Monday 7 December 1914, inviting civic representatives of local towns and industry (including Waynman Dixon) to join them. After lengthy discussions, the raising of the Teesside Battalion, with 1,100 men, was confirmed. The battalion would be attached to the Yorkshire Regiment, with headquarters in Middlesbrough. Men currently enlisting could opt to choose the Teesside Battalion as their preferred unit, but training would not begin until the New Year. Various correspondence followed between the mayor and the War Office regarding administrative matters, including the minimum height for recruits which the War Office insisted must be 5ft 3in (1.6m).

To encourage recruitment, arrangements would be made regarding men employed in key local industries, and professional footballers joining up would be granted leave to play on a Saturday if possible. Two days later, Alderman Alfred Mattison, a former Middlesbrough player, addressed the players after training to point out that with the Teesside Battalion now being formed 'it would be grand if the Middlesbrough players went forward as a whole'. A minute from the Middlesbrough Football Club board meeting, 10 December 1914, affirms the decision that, in the event of any players joining the Teesside Battalion, the club would fully honour their contracts. Manager, Tom McIntosh, wasn't so fortunate, as the club decided on 4 January 1915 that they would only pay him half-salary for the rest of his contract if he joined up.

With Middlesbrough town clerk, Preston Kitchen, already receiving letters from men wanting to join the battalion, it became imperative to appoint a commanding officer. The first person interviewed, on Saturday 12 December, was Colonel the Hon. W. L. Vane, brother of Lord Barnard, who was stationed at the Barracks, Newcastle. Although the mayor was confident Vane would accept the position, a period of anxious waiting followed as

Vane was also being considered for another post. Two weeks later, on 24 December 1914, a telegram arrived from Vane: 'Much regret no answer from War Office so unable to accept your invitation.'

Wasting no time, the mayor immediately sent the following telegram to Major Becher, Duke of Wellington Regiment, the Barracks, in Halifax:

> War office approved formation of Teesside Battalion 1,200 to 1,300 men. Colonel Watson General Officer Commanding York suggest your name to me as most suitable person to accept appointment of Commanding Officer.

This image is particularly interesting because it includes Lt Colonel H.W. Becher, who was asked to lead the Teesside Battalion when it was first raised. The postcard is the standard reply that was sent out to those who applied to join the battalion.

Major Becher sent his acceptance the next day adding, in a personal letter to the mayor on Saturday 26 December 1914, that he hoped that they would not expect too much of him as since having resigned his commission in 1907, he had been out of the army as a reserve for eight years. In fact Becher, with over twenty years' military experience, including war service in South Africa 1900–02, proved to be a good appointment, remaining with the battalion until it ceased to exist in 1918.

The first 'Monster Recruiting Meeting' for the Teesside Battalion took place at 8 p.m. on Wednesday, 6 January 1915. A letter from Town Clerk Preston Kitchen, to Chief Constable Henry Riches, noted that 'the mayor was anxious to make a big success of this meeting'. The flood of recruits in the early days of the war had slowed and it was important to recover numbers.

The well-managed evening began when a procession made up of local bands and military personnel, including some walking wounded from Hemlington Hospital, left the quadrangle at the Town Hall at 7 p.m. to proceed through the principal streets of the town before arriving back at the Town Hall. On the platform that evening were British and Belgian wounded, as well as civic dignitaries from Middlesbrough, including Alderman Alfred Mattison who had recently returned from driving the Middlesbrough ambulance to the Western Front. Joining them were representatives from other local urban councils. To provide an appropriate mood the borough organist, Felix Corbett, played a number of 'patriotic selections' throughout the evening.

The mayor explained with great pride that, not wanting Middlesbrough to be behind other industrial centres with their own battalions, he had obtained permission from the War Office to raise a local battalion to be known as the 12th (Service) Battalion of the Yorkshire Regiment, attached to the 123rd Brigade. The battalion would be based at Marton Hall, leased from Carl Ferdinand Bolckow of Torquay, at a cost of £300 per year, beginning 1 January 1915. Loud applause greeted his announcement that members of Middlesbrough Football Club: club secretary & manager, Tom McIntosh, and the players, Joseph Hisbent, George Malcolm, Harry Cook and Richard Wynn, had agreed to enlist too.

Two MP's, John Butcher, member for York, and William Pringle, member for north-west Lanarkshire, gave speeches stressing why young men should join the new battalion. When Councillor Spence finished the evening with an allusion to the Teesside Battalion one day marching through the streets of Berlin, over 200 young men came forward to enlist, adding their names to the 100 applications already received for the new battalion. Three days later, Robert Nelson Hermiston, aged 38, a schoolmaster and councillor from

The insignia of the Teesside Battalion – note the pickaxe and the rifle reflecting their role as a Pioneer Battalion.

Normanby, became the first member of the Teesside Battalion after being sworn in by the mayor.

An intense local recruiting campaign began with a widespread poster campaign. The appointments of various officers to the battalion, including new commissions as well as the transfer of men from various other regiments, were completed. The applications for commissions in the new battalion show the fervent desire of local men to join the new battalion. The youngest applicant was just 19, whilst the oldest was 48. Reasons for joining varied, including 'I have studied and learnt the 1914 edition of *Infantry Training*', 'being from Middlesbrough', 'my employers will only release me for service if get a commission' and 'I am personally acquainted with the mayor'. The mayor was even asked if he thought the pay would be enough for the lifestyle of an officer.

Applications to join as a private recognised the ethos behind the pal's battalions, with friends making joint applications in the same letter. One application from two friends, Fred Duckett and John Causier, was withdrawn when Waynman Dixon, director of Raylton, Dixon & Co. Ltd, refused them permission to enlist. The mayor kindly wrote a letter of thanks for 'their desire to help their country'.

Many applications were straight to the point. Harold Savage of 108A Newport Road wrote that he was 'quite willing to joine [*sic*] the New tees side Battalion of Earl Kitchener's army. I was 18 years last March'. While 20-year-old William Hayes of 19 Adam Street, one of five brothers living with his mother Ada, sent a postcard with 'Will join your Teesside Battalion' written on the back. More unusual applications included those from men concerned that having no top set of teeth would be a barrier to enlisting – one applicant wrote a whole page on this subject.

Marton Hall, Home from Home

Marton Hall Estate, once owned by the prominent local iron master H.W.F. Bolckow, was recommended for billeting purposes. A group from Middlesbrough Town Council, which examined the site on 7 September 1914, reported that with some alterations to the infrastructure, e.g. laying on gas for heating, it could quite comfortably billet 1,000 men.

It was an important milestone in raising the battalion's local profile when the first batch of men arrived at Marton Hall on Tuesday, 9 February 1915. With the comfort of the men paramount, the *North-Eastern Daily Gazette* enthused over the new training depot, describing it as 'being located in very pleasant countryside … a gratifying change for the soldiers, as most come from industrial areas [and] when spring comes it will be particularly pleasant'.

There was space for 550 men inside the hall, with accommodation for the rest in the stables which had been suitably altered for this purpose. The men, who were each allocated four blankets, slept in a bed rather than on floorboards. Officers were quartered at the hall, whilst a large mess room for 450 men had been erected in the quadrangle of the stables for the ordinary soldiers.

After a thirty minute lecture the men enjoyed free time each evening. They were also free on Saturday afternoons and on Sundays, after church parade. The *North-Eastern Daily Gazette* said that the battalion had made an excellent start with 'good officers, fine quarters, healthy surroundings … splendid equipment, plain well-cooked food and every provision for the comfort of the troops'. A YMCA hut, donated by Mrs Howard, opened on 24 March 1915. Erected and furnished at a cost of £400 and run by Henry Shorter, it offered tea and coffee at subsidised prices, along with reading and writing facilities. Every evening ended with a hymn, and concerts were held regularly and were popular with both the Teesside Battalion and the Royal Engineers, who also trained there. When Shorter moved on to Winchester, George Wood took over and the popularity of the centre increased further. In fact, when the facility closed shortly after the war ended, many ex-soldiers returned to attend a memorable concert and evening of reminiscing.

Y.M.C.A. HUT, TEESSIDE BATTALION, MARTON HALL.

The YMCA hut in the grounds of Marton Hall was a much-loved institution for men from the Teesside Battalion who were training there. It provided many different facilities. A group of local dignitaries pose here including the mayor and Lt Colonel H.W. Becher. (Author's collection)

Almost unnoticed in the press report (possibly overshadowed by news of a pay increase of 2*d* (1p) a day for rank and file) was the news that the War Office had 'intimated that it would recognise this new force as a Pioneer Battalion', not as an infantry which had been the original intention. This change, part of the War Office's strategy announced in December 1914, aimed to develop divisional pioneer battalions to support the infantry. The reaction of volunteers is not documented, although Middlesbrough's MP, Penry Williams, approved having himself set an example by accepting a commission in a similar unit in Gloucestershire.

Training continued at Marton Hall throughout the spring of 1915, with few problems except for the unfortunate death of one trainee from South Bank following a brief illness. (Although the boy's family thought otherwise, the coroner ruled there was no medical negligence or fault in the medical care available for men stationed at Marton.) Despite being 269 short of their target of 1,100 recruits, the battalion was ordered to move to Gosforth in April 1915. However, this was postponed following a request from the mayor who was still anxious to meet the recruitment target, with a 'big recruiting rally' arranged for Thursday, 29 April 1915, at Middlesbrough Town Hall.

It was hoped that the presence of Middlesbrough's first recipient of the Victoria Cross, Private James Smith, would encourage further recruitment. It was certainly an opportunity for the town to show their admiration of his bravery. Everyone present stood up and sang 'For he's a jolly good fellow' and the mayor, on behalf of Cleveland Ironmasters and the Town Council, presented Smith with a purse of gold. The presence of Smith persuaded forty-seven men to enlist on the night – a successful evening, considering that only 109 men had enlisted in the previous two weeks.

Following their eventual move to Gosforth on 10 May 1915, the battalion strength reached 1,040

Pioneer battalions were support units for the men at the front line. Once the trenches became established in autumn 1914, the infantry required support labour to manage their maintenance. Pioneers differed from normal infantry in that, although capable of fighting, they were a mix of skilled and labouring men.

The Teesside Battalion on parade outside Marton Hall in the spring of 1915. (Courtesy of Teesside Archive)

Looking north towards Middlesbrough, a wonderful panoramic vista still recognisable today. (Courtesy of Teesside Archive)

Officers of the Teesside Battalion and their families, around March 1915. Colonel Becher is on the far left of the image standing next to Sir Hugh Bell. They are grouped outside the entrance to Marton Hall, which is already showing signs of decay from being the magnificent building it once was. (Courtesy of Teesside Archive)

A recruitment poster from June 1915. Before Lord Derby's scheme and military conscription, the Recruitment Committee was very active in promoting recruitment. (Courtesy of Teesside Archive)

men, boosted by men from other regiments. Middlesbrough Football Club, having had an official photo taken of manager Tom McIntosh and those players in the Teesside Battalion, presented each of them with a framed copy. Later that summer, on 13 August 1915, the Teesside Battalion left the north-east for further training, including spells at Cannock Chase where they made a camp on Penkridge Bank, Badajos Barracks, Aldershot and then in December 1915, Pirbright near Woking in Surrey for musketry training. Whilst at Aldershot, they had joined the 40th (Bantam) Division as the Divisional Pioneer Battalion. This meant that, as well as their pioneer duties, they would be expected to fight if the need arose.

Having completed their training by the middle of May 1916, the Teesside Battalion was part of a review at 'Laffans Plain' by King George V, where he commented on the great credit the battalion brought to Teesside.

Finally, on 1 June 1916, they embarked at Southampton for France and the Western Front.

National Registration

Back in Middlesbrough, with the upper age limit having been raised to 40 in May 1915, recruitment meetings continued throughout the summer. The mayor and the Recruitment Committee undertook the raising of 1,017 recruits for the 14th (Reserve) Battalion Yorkshire Regiment (composed of depot companies of the 12th Service Battalion – the Teesside Pioneers Battalion). The campaign opened on 16 October 1915 with a march through the town to the old Market Place, where a stand was set up complete with a Union Jack, and vocal appeals made for men. As recruitment numbers continued to fall throughout the summer it was clear that intervention from central government was required. The National Registration Act of July 1915, an assessment of the number of men between the ages of 15 and 65 employed in each trade, underlined this need when it disclosed that almost 5 million males of military age were not in the military forces.

The Derby Scheme and Conscription

Lord Derby, the director general of recruiting from 11 October 1915, brought in the 'Derby Scheme'. Men were asked to attest their willingness to serve, on the understanding that they would be called up only when necessary, and that single men would be called up before married volunteers.

Administering this scheme generated a great deal of paperwork and man hours, with recruiting offices in Middlesbrough being open until 11 p.m. as the deadline for registration approached. When the scheme closed, on 15 December 1915, over 1 million single men across the country had still not enlisted. In Middlesbrough 4,212 men were described as enlisted or attested, from a total of 6,958 (60.5 per cent), with 1,106 men (15.9 per cent) refusing to enlist. The other 1,640 men (23.6 per cent) were not eligible for recruitment.

The national data eventually led to the Military Service Act of 27 January 1916, which announced that conscription for men aged 18–41 would begin on 2 March 1916. Exemptions included men who were married, widowed with children, serving in the Royal Navy, a member of the clergy, or working in one of the reserved occupations such as munitions. The Act was modified in May 1916 to include married men, and again in 1918 when the upper age limit was extended to 51.

The advent of the Derby Scheme and conscription saw the introduction, in Middlesbrough on 10 March 1916, of the Military Service Tribunals to which men could apply for exemption from military service. Tribunals listened to claims for exemption, then upheld or dismissed the claim. Although they dealt with many different types of cases, their reputation and legacy has remained controversial because of their treatment of 'conscientious objectors'. There were two 'Courts of Military Tribunals' in Middlesbrough. Mayor J. Calvert presided over Court A, and Alderman W.J. Bruce over Court B. It is claimed that, unlike other tribunals, whose tendency was to hand objectors over immediately to the military, there was a 'genuine desire [in Middlesbrough] to discriminate within the limits of discrimination provided by the law'.

A certificate of registration from autumn 1915. (Courtesy of the Dorman Museum)

NATIONAL REGISTER

Authority is given to

to call upon men who, according to the National Register, are eligible for enlistment.

Chairman of Committee.

Derby.

October............th, 1915.

Director of Recruiting.

Over 400 cases were heard on the first day. The court was held at Middlesbrough, with Mayor J. Calvert JP presiding and Lt Col Gibson Poole and Mr Hustler sitting as military representatives. Twelve members usually made up the tribunal. Preston Kitchen, the town clerk, read out the conditions of service before proceedings began. Over the period when the tribunal sat, every possible reason for exemption seemed to be given. The work of the tribunal could not have succeeded without the advisory committee who examined the cases, dividing them into those related to occupation and those requested for other reasons.

One of the first applications was from a cinematograph proprietor, Ernest Smith, for his two employees. He claimed that they were needed because one 'played the organ and piano [whilst] the other was trusted with confidential secrets'. When asked why he couldn't employ women who had been trained for the same job, Smith replied that 'women were not dependable and would … become panic stricken in an emergency'. The application was refused.

Some claimants were given time to sort out their affairs; a master boot maker was given three months to close down his business. Even Red Cross workers were not exempt. In October 1916 a male section leader in the Voluntary Aid Detachment, British Red Cross Society (No 29 Yorks), asked for release from call-up. The British Red Cross said the man was their most dependable person, and had met over 2,000 wounded soldiers as they arrived at Middlesbrough Station before supervising their journey to Hemlington Hospital. He also taught first aid, nursing and hygiene to more than fifty people each week. In recognition of this work, he was given three months exemption until January 1917. Among others granted exemption was a timber merchant's clerk, who claimed he was the sole means of support for his 76-year-old widowed mother and her 72-year-old sister.

Things didn't always go smoothly. On 17 March 1916, the military representative at the Middlesbrough Rural Military Court, J.W. Pennyman, protested that at the previous hearing not one of the thirty-four cases heard had resulted in the man being sent to the Front. He urged the tribunal to remember that 'there was a serious war going on and that men were needed'. Many of these were men working on farms, and decisions were always difficult in such cases, when the importance of the food supply was always a consideration and replacement labour not always able to be found quickly. Men who owned one-man businesses were also very difficult to judge, as they often had very genuine cases – yet, aware of the need for more men, it was difficult to find in their favour.

As the demand for men increased throughout 1916, so did the work of the tribunals, with over 4,000 applications for exemption being made. In one week in May, 850 cases were heard at the two Middlesbrough courts. On 10 July 1916, fourteen conscientious objectors were court-martialled and sentenced, at Richmond Castle, to 112 days' imprisonment. When there were cases heard at Middlesbrough based on religious reasons, the applicant was usually given a non-combatant role. A wharf labourer asked for exemption because he was the only one left to keep the home together. It was then pointed out to him that he lived alone! The application was refused.

3

SAFE IN YOUR BED

'Don't Panic, Lady'

Across the country, towns like Middlesbrough found themselves caught in the maelstrom of war. Daily life for the ordinary person in Middlesbrough had changed very quickly and, having proudly sent their men off to fight, there was now the urgent task of managing life at home and contributing to the collective national aim of defeating the enemy. Middlesbrough Borough Council played a supportive role in this process despite a change in civic leader on 9 November 1915, when Joseph S. Calvert replaced William J. Bruce, who had served as mayor for two years. Calvert, born in Middlesbrough in 1853, was a popular choice and he showed strong leadership of the town throughout his four years of office.

A priority for Mayor W.J. Bruce in August 1914 had been to ensure an affordable efficient food supply was available for all. On the very first day of war, Wednesday 5 August, a special meeting of the Middlesbrough General Purpose Committee decided that this was so important that it needed a sub-committee with the sole aim of safeguarding food supplies. The immediate problems facing the committee were short supplies, panic buying and resultant hoarding. As heavy demand led to price increases, feelings ran high, with allegations made that shopkeepers were raising the prices of necessities in order to make a large profit. Accusations that shopkeepers were being unpatriotic triggered angry exchanges with customers. Shopkeepers were called 'worse enemies than the Germans' at one local council meeting. Numerous complaints were made to 'Weights and Measures' at the Town Hall. Preston Kitchen, the town clerk, tried to calm the situation down by issuing a statement that the prices charged by retailers only reflected the prices at wholesalers.

Many of the problems with food supply were self-imposed, through panic buying. Amos Hinton & Sons who, as one of Middlesbrough's main food merchants, had sold a month's supply of flour in five days, blamed their customers. Issuing a statement, they said they had no wish to profit from the situation, but also said that customers needed to take some responsibility and not hoard food. Those with excess food were asked to either sell it or give it away to those in need, but there is little evidence that this happened. In fact, the hoarding which had been so evident in the last few days of peace continued, with reports of people buying 10 stones (63.5kg) of flour in a week compared to the normal order of 1 stone (6.35kg).

A selection of advertisements hoping to persuade the Middlesbrough public that the panic over food in August 1914 was at an end. (Courtesy of the Evening Gazette, *Middlesbrough)*

Any sort of credit was frowned upon, regarded as unworkable by the wholesalers and the grocers, with both parties insisting on cash only when the goods were purchased. Heavy criticism was made of the 'middle classes' who possessed the financial means to purchase food in large quantities – newspapers reported examples of people going to the warehouses with motor vehicles and purchasing large quantities far beyond their needs. They could pay

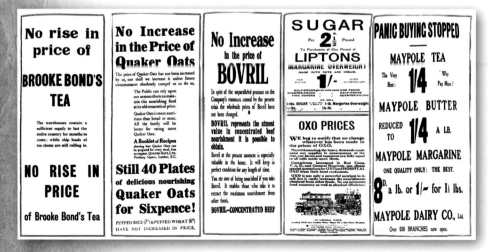

cash, and this meant that the warehouses were willing to do business with them. With the situation failing to improve, the mayor made another public appeal for people not to buy food to stockpile, and for tradesmen not to sell large quantities to any customer, as this would only make the situation worse.

By mid-August the panic concerning food supplies was beginning to stabilise, as people settled down into a routine. The price of flour had reduced to 1*s* 8*d* (8p) per stone, after hitting 2*s* 6*d* (12.5p) only three weeks previously, and there was less acrimony between food merchants and customer. The problems with the food supply would return later in the war when unrestricted submarine activity had a drastic impact on the merchant shipping bringing imports of food to Britain. This necessitated the rationing of some foodstuffs in 1918 to ensure that Britain did not starve – a drastic but effective action.

'We've Come for the Horses'

There were other problems, however. The military purchased many of the best horses across the area, both heavy and light draught animals, for use as army remounts. Horses were so important to the war effort that thousands were imported from abroad to boost numbers. Nearly 1 million horses were taken, across the country, with only an estimated 65,000 returning.

This often caused a great deal of upset. At High Grange Farm, Billingham, the twenty horses owned by farmer Frederick Bell were his pride and joy. His 11-year-old daughter, Freda, recalled two army officers calling at 5 p.m. on a dark October evening to say that they had come for the horses. An animated conversation followed before the men left. The next day they returned and the horses were gone, including Bell's best hunter. Seventy years later, Freda still recalled the tears in her father's eyes – the only time she ever saw him cry.

It wasn't just farms that were affected – Middlesbrough Corporation, the NER, the Co-operative Society and local carting contractors all lost many of their best horses. Many shops had problems with transporting goods, particularly for delivery. The Sanitary Authorities in Middlesbrough couldn't carry out their work due to the lack of horses, and asked the public if they could help the scavenging of the town by burning their own dry refuse. The directors of Redcar Race Company informed the War Office that they had offered the use of all stables at the racecourse to the commander-in-chief of the Northern Command.

The value of horses can be gauged by an episode concerning John Gettins, the bridge master at the Transporter Bridge over the Tees, who personally worked the Transporter Bridge car over the river at 3 a.m. to carry forage across the river for the military to feed their horses.

Down at the Allotment

The problems surrounding the food supply placed greater importance on any foods that could be grown at home. Even before the 1908 Allotments Act, allotments were popular in Middlesbrough. A plot at Ayresome Grange Farm in Middlesbrough could be rented for 15*s* (75p) a year, a sum that could be repaid many times over in the supply of extra food.

Allotments became even more important during wartime. A letter to the *North-Eastern Daily Gazette* suggested it would be a wise policy if all available garden land was cultivated, and seeds sown for autumn/winter crops, in preparation for a lengthy war. The mayor issued a notice directing small areas of land to be used for the growing of crops to meet any forthcoming shortages in food supplies. Newspaper articles regularly printed advice on growing vegetables and other food. During the war, 499 acres were under cultivation by 3,318 tenants, including 102 acres of open spaces owned by the council.

Despite farms being vital in food production, many farmers lost labourers who had enlisted. One suggestion was to use some of the large number of the unemployed riverside men to help with agricultural work in the surrounding district. Villages like

Nunthorpe had a system whereby men could leave their name and address with the Assistant Overseer of the Parish, so that farmers who required help could contact them. Casual labour brought in extra money for families too. Although the Military Tribunal did occasionally allow exemption for farm workers, it was the Women's Land Army, formed in 1917 that would prove vital to farmers at a time when the supply of men had decreased even further.

Closed Today

Retailers in Middlesbrough soon made use of the war to promote their goods – within two days of war starting, Ross's Clothiers in Linthorpe Road were advertising their 'Great War Sale'. Others followed them, and it was not very long before many advertisements adopted a war theme. With market conditions constantly changing, traders needed to adapt quickly or face ruin. They too had their problems caused by the war. As utility costs increased due to the war, it was announced on 14 September 1914 that shops across the town would be closing earlier to reduce lighting expenses. This meant that they would close at 7 p.m. on four nights and at 9 p.m. on Saturday, with Wednesday being Half Day closing at 1 p.m.

Many local companies faced grim problems at the start of the war. There had been virtually no business in the town on Tuesday 4 August, and ships that had loaded up with pig iron were being asked to unload it back at Middlesbrough. The Middlesbrough Exchange opened for business on Wednesday, 5 August, but the few traders that attended discussed nothing but the war. A.J. Dorman, head of Dorman, Long and Co. Ltd, issued a statement that they would be making 'every possible effort to keep the works going and thus maintain their men in employment.' Optimism was drawn from the hope that whilst trade with Northern Europe would be hit, trade with the Empire would still continue and help companies remain in business.

It was worrying, nevertheless. In the first week of war, two iron works in Stockton were closing down, a furnace was damped down at Linthorpe Ironworks and men on one of the furnaces at Bell Iron works were given fourteen days' notice. The mayor made a public appeal for employers to continue business for as long as possible, and to try to ensure that labourers, at least, remained in work. Nevertheless, many were quickly laid off, particularly riverside workers.

In the iron industry, trade was marginally better as firms kept going in the hope of orders from the anticipated heavy demand for iron and steel products for naval and military purposes. With Britain cut off entirely from Continental competition, British manufacturers survived on orders from home consumers. Although all overseas trade was halted pending the navy securing safety for British shipping, once this was achieved British manufacturers could trade without any German competition.

Selling prices rose – the Middlesbrough Exchange reported that steel ship plates and angles had risen by £1 per ton and all other finished iron and steel goods had gone up by 10s (50p) per ton. However, this had to be offset against the rise in the cost of raw materials. The strong demand for pig iron from home consumers, contrasted with export trade for pig iron being down. Continental manufacturers were the keenest rivals, but they had also been the best customers. Shipments of pig iron dropped to 31,870 tons, the lowest figure since December 1900 (42,230 tons) when Continental ports were icebound. In July, 82,412 tons had been shipped, compared with a total of 168,133 tons shipped in August 1913.

Industry began to recover slowly towards the end of August. Local ironworks reported improved trading and shipyards were once again starting to offer regular work. Trade routes opened once again and shipping seemed to be on the move. It was announced that the Spanish iron ore ships had started to trade with Middlesbrough again which would help keep the works going. The Japanese liner, *Maru*, originally bound for Antwerp, had arrived on the Tees. Casual workers, especially riverside workers, the employees hit hardest when war began, also found conditions improving by the end of August.

Guard the River

The fear of invasion invoked tight security procedures. The chief constable, Henry Riches, was responsible for security and, having reassured the Town Council, was keen to exercise his control. The *North-Eastern Daily Gazette* reported that:

> Only an hour after the declaration of war, there were exciting scenes at Dent's Wharf, Middlesbrough. The tramp, tramp, of a posse of police, including the Chief Constable, arrived at the SS *Minotas* shouting 'Halt! The men marched up the gangway and arrested in the King's name, the ship and ship's company of ten Germans, two Russian Finns, two Assyrians and a British subject. The ship was then escorted at 3 a.m., under the charge of a Tees pilot and secured at Middlesbrough Dock.

Two other vessels detained that same night were the *Emma Winloss*, a German boat with a cargo of iron to discharge, and an English steamer, SS *Neophyte*, which had a cargo of pig iron bound for Hamburg.

On Thursday, 6 August, Tees Commissioners published updated regulations for entering the Port of Tees. These were aimed at increasing security on the river to prevent mines being laid, or the river entrance being blocked by the sinking of a vessel. Shipping entering the river would be subject to inspection by the examination steamer, *William Fallows*. If any incoming vessel refused to comply, a signal would be sent to the batteries stationed at the entrance to the river and a shot would be fired across the vessel's bows. Any further refusal to comply would result in guns on both sides of the river opening fire. From October 1914, a licensed local pilot was required to go on board before each vessel entered the river. Warnings were issued to fishermen that they should not leave the river between sunset and sunrise, or they too would run the risk of being fired upon by the land batteries.

On the evening of Sunday, 9 August, a soldier guarding the riverbank close to Eston Jetty challenged six youths who had taken a rowing boat out on the Tees. When they failed to answer him, he fired his gun at them! The youths quickly returned to the riverbank where, having established their identities, they were issued with a severe caution.

Although procedures were reported to be working well, with only a few vessels failing to comply, security around the river was tightened still further on 18 August, when the River Tees was put under martial law as far upriver as Stockton Bridge, resulting in all bridges and jetties being closely guarded. There was often great public interest in the changing of the guard at the Middlesbrough Exchange and the Transporter Bridge, where many were impressed by 'the Territorials lining up in smart style with fixed bayonets'.

It's Cold at the South Gare

As winter approached, the military, guarding the entrance to the river, faced many long cold hours manning the lookout post at the South Gare. The public were asked to show their support by donating newspapers and illustrated magazines, leaving them in boxes placed on the platform of Redcar Station for distribution. Later, donations included warm items of clothing for soldiers during the harsh conditions of the winter months.

A letter dated 27 September 1914, from 'Robert Lownder Aspinall, Lt Col, 3rd Battalion APWO, Yorkshire Regiment, Commanding Troops, South Gare' to Mrs Claude Pease at the Red Cross Guild, records his thanks for the 'most welcome gifts of shirts and socks sent to the men of the South Gare Breakwater Defence'. He had written at the request of the men who he commanded. The *North-Eastern Daily Gazette*, on 30 January 1915, reported that a great deal of football was played to while away the long hours off-duty. The latest game between the Royal Engineers and the 3rd Yorkshires had ended with the Engineers winning 2–0. The pitch, which was on the open sands next to the breakwater, had homemade goalposts and was described as being very heavy.

Who Goes There?

As well as the fear of invasion, the expectation of a naval engagement off the coast led to fears for the safety of coastal towns like Saltburn and Redcar, bringing a strong military presence to both. An unfortunate incident occurred at Saltburn on 21 August 1914. A holidaymaker, Thomas Taylor, aged 22, of Hull, was riding a motorbike along the promenade close to midnight when he was challenged three or four times by a sentry on guard. When he failed to respond the sentry shot him dead. After the inquest established that the challenges had been lawfully made, the coroner said in his summary that the sentry, having seen a light, followed instructions to challenge three times and then fire. Although soldiers were told to fire low, it wasn't always easy to be certain of doing so in the total darkness of night. Whilst this was an unfortunate case of Taylor probably being unable to hear the challenges rather than posing a threat to the authorities, this was 'at the risk of rider, for a sentry was not supposed to

A booklet to commemorate the bombardment by German ships of Hartlepool, Whitby and Scarborough in December 1914. (Courtesy of the Dorman Museum)

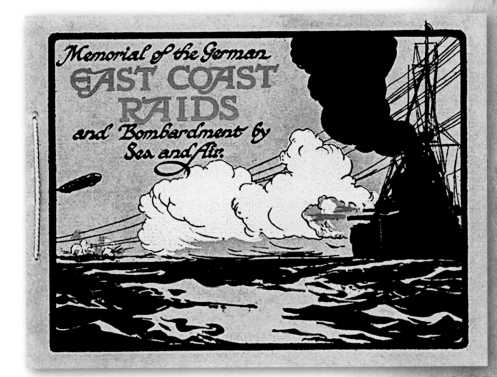

The extent of the damage can be seen in this view of Moor Terrace, Hartlepool, following the bombardment. (Courtesy of the Dorman Museum)

discriminate'. The coroner concluded that it was 'an unfortunate affair', expressed his sympathy to the relatives but added 'this is one of the matters that must be faced in war'.

With the continuous stream of official warnings and reports, it was not surprising that some people living at the coast said they were living in a constant state of apprehension. Reports in August stated a number of war vessels had been seen off the coast at Marske and Saltburn, although they were some distance away. Inhabitants living near the coast were officially warned of the risk they ran if the Germans landed. They were told to head for the countryside, or remain in their homes at their own risk.

A much happier event involving the security forces featured a destroyer that was patrolling the Cleveland coast on 9 October, calling at Saltburn. Several officers with business in town came ashore in a small boat, whilst many residents viewed the boat from the pier and the Boy Scouts, who were helping the coast-guards, enjoyed being taken on board to see the ship.

One Morning in December 1914

Many people in Middlesbrough heard the bombardment of Hartlepool by the German Navy, which killed 127 people on 16 December 1914. Some were woken by the noise, while others felt the windows in their houses or offices rattling. Many witnessed the three German battlecruisers firing from their position off Tees Bay. North of the river, Gwen Nielsen who lived at Billingham Hall, wrote in her diary of a stream of refugees walking along the road from Wolviston, pulling handcarts piled high with possessions.

The event served to confirm the need for the continued security of the Tees and coastal communities. The defences of the Tees were strengthened even further, with more powerful guns and additional training battalions, leading to almost 12,000 men being employed for this purpose by 1918. There were fifteen anti-aircraft stations within an area stretching from Crimdon in the north to Skinningrove in the south. A submarine base was established at Eston with wharves and petrol tank facilities, allowing submarines to enter the North Sea from the Tees. Airfields at Redcar and Marske both played their part in the war, providing facilities for air-defence as well as air-offence.

The Police and the Boy Scouts

Maintaining day-to-day policing in Middlesbrough was difficult in wartime, particularly as eleven constables were immediately called up. Additional duties meant officers found that all leave was cancelled, and they were being asked to work shifts of at least twelve hours a day.

To ease the situation, the chief constable sent a circular letter out to police pensioners, with fourteen of them responding to this appeal for their assistance in strengthening the force. Many were pleased to be involved, but some duties could be irritating. A constable on riverside duty at Middlesbrough reported that the rats were so numerous that 'for safety's sake [he was] obliged to tie up the bottoms of his trousers with string'. He also reported that the stench from the drain at the fish warehouse was so unbearable that he had to 'leave the Landing at frequent intervals for fresh air'.

A letter from the Secretary of State, on 17 August 1914, requested that the chief constable ensure that steps had been taken for the 'continuous preservation of order during the War'. This included the sanctioning and coordinating of the use of Special Constables and other voluntary forces, including 'Motor Patrols and Boy Scouts'. However, volunteer helpers acting 'on their own account' should be strongly discouraged, to avoid confusion and difficulty.

After a letter from the district commissioner in Middlesbrough, confirming their employment, a coordinated use of local Boy Scouts began, which proved to be of great assistance. Under the control of the police, and only using boys with their parents' consent, the Scouts performed a range of duties including watching telegraphs and bridges as well as carrying dispatches. Others were employed in running messages at the Town Hall or helping local farmers with harvesting. Those acting as lookouts on the Cleveland coast were said to be really enjoying camping out on the cliff tops. Early in the war the Middlesbrough Scouting Association even tried to form patrols of former Scouts; those who had passed the 'Second Class Test' were invited to apply to the Scout headquarters in Church Street. The Boy Scouts were in such demand that Middlesbrough Council made a financial donation towards new uniforms after a letter from the local secretary in October 1914.

Volunteer Training Corps, the Civil Guard and Zeppelins

With the fear of invasion, many patriotic citizens were desperate to be involved in the war effort, particularly ex-military men no longer able to join the military. There was a call to revive the old 'Volunteer Force', with service given free and the cost of arms and equipment met by private or public subscription. The Volunteer Training Corps, with Sir Hugh Bell as president, was formed in December 1914 to defend the area if there was an invasion. There was concern that it would take men from the Front, but this was largely unfounded.

Although the War Office was hesitant at first, the venture continued. The three corps included one from Dorman Long and Co. who erected a Drill Hall in Oxford Road, which later became the Dorman Social and Athletic Club. In March 1915 the three corps amalgamated, and became part of the North Riding Regiment of Volunteers. With 1,100 men having joined there were now two corps, with two commandants, F.J. Forster JP and Captain William Bunn.

This cartoon from 29 March 1915 captures perfectly the review of the Middlesbrough Volunteer Force. In the era of photographs in newspapers being rare, these cartoons often depicted events, particularly football games. (Courtesy of the Evening Gazette, Middlesbrough)

With police numbers reduced, there was strong support for a local Civil Guard. Inspector Seymour of the Middlesbrough Police had agreed to train the men, and the rifle range in the Municipal Buildings had been booked for target practice. However, the War Office initially refused to sanction the idea because it could compromise recruitment for Kitchener's Army.

The idea was successfully revived at the end of October, when 800 enthusiastic people formed the new Civil Guard. The members, initially organised in twenty companies of approximately forty people, assisted the policing of the town though they would have no powers of arrest. On 28 March 1915 the Civil Guard had the entire responsibility for policing the town between 6 a.m. and 9 p.m. Each man had a badge, truncheon, warrant card and armlet, and their duties comprised of guarding public buildings, railway bridges etc. They also had the important duty of ensuring that the town was kept in darkness in case of Zeppelin raids. A motorcycle section of over fifty members were also formed.

Zeppelin L34 caught in the searchlights on 27 November 1916, the night it was shot down over Tees Bay. (Courtesy of the Dorman Museum)

When Zeppelin raids began in 1915, procedures to cope were already in place. It was said that, despite the glow from industry, on receiving the order 'Take Air Raid Action' all lights from the blast furnaces and the area around it, could be extinguished within twelve minutes. Aircraft from the Air Station at Redcar were usually sent up to check on any lights being visible. Although it is said that this procedure saved the town on several occasions, there were some bombs that got through.

On the night of 8/9 September 1915, a Zeppelin dropped bombs at the mouth of the River Tees. Zeppelin activity was increased again on Saturday 1 April 1916, with a heavy raid by Zeppelin *L11* along the north-east coast and many casualties in Sunderland.

Middlesbrough got off lightly, two bombs being dropped in a field at Cargo Fleet causing damage, mainly broken windows, to a hotel, school, two shops and 115 houses. Port Clarence and the Transporter Bridge also came under attack. In a lucky escape, a bomb was seen to fall between the structure's steel girders before dropping safely into the River Tees. The most spectacular memories people have are of the Zeppelin being caught in the searchlights, with the noise of their engines said to resemble the noise of a train in a tunnel. Many people also remember the Zeppelin *L34* being shot down on 27 November 1916, by 2nd Lt Ian Pyott DSO of 36 Squadron Seaton Carew, at West Hartlepool, where it crashed in flames into Tees Bay at 11.40 p.m. Kapitanleutnant Max Konrad Dietrich and all his crew were reported killed.

When the King and Queen visited the town on 14 June 1917, the Civil Guard had the honour of lining their route in the town.

Spies Everywhere

The threat of invasion fuelled paranoia about 'aliens' and German spies. Various edicts regularly warned the public to be on their guard for spies or suspicious activity.

Some were reminiscent of the Home Guard in the Second World War. The *Whitby Gazette* instructed the public to look out for any suspicious-looking people walking along the cliff tops, adding that if they could not say 'th' (and presumably 'w') properly, they were, in all probability, German. A man enjoying a solitary walk along a Cleveland cliff top, found himself under arrest and having to explain his actions.

Pigeons were also under suspicion. Anyone finding a pigeon with foreign rings on their legs or foreign marks on their wings

For those who wished to help with the war but who were not eligible for military service, a Voluntary Services Bureau was established to help put them in touch with organisations where they could be useful. Inspired by this, over 100 tradesmen of the town met at Hinton's Café at the end of September and formed the Middlesbrough and District Tradesmen Emergency Training Corps. Headed by Captain Bunn, they gave military drill, rifle shooting and ambulance training to tradesmen, their assistants and clerks in retail establishments.

was told to retain it and immediately contact the War Office. When Thomas Warrener of Pearl Street, Middlesbrough, found that a pigeon from Antwerp had entered his loft in mid-August this caused great concern as to its purpose, but no ulterior motive was ever found.

Aliens from Middlesbrough

The many foreign nationals, or 'aliens' as they were termed, living in Middlesbrough posed a problem for the authorities, particularly those of German origins or with German family connections. At the start of the First World War, the Alien Registration Act and British Nationality Act of 1914 required all aliens over 16 to register at local police stations and to demonstrate a good character and knowledge of English. Notices were duly posted around the town clearly stating the procedure for the registration of all aliens.

The authorities were quick to act. On the evening of Friday, 7 August, the 'quiet arrest' took place under the supervision of the chief constable, of all the male Germans remaining in Middlesbrough who were not naturalised. There were emotional scenes when the men were forcibly taken from their families, as several had been born in Middlesbrough or, being naturalised, had lived in the town for many years owning a local business that contributed to the community. They considered themselves to be more British than German – many were very bitter about the Kaiser and certainly had no desire to return to Germany. The arrests included Mr Abraham, minister of the German Church, and several members of the Lorch family, the world famous Risley act who were appearing that week on stage at the Hippodrome.

The 'prisoners of war' were locked overnight in the Town Hall crypt, under a strong police guard, awaiting instructions from the authorities. They would normally have been sent to York Castle, but after a long Saturday afternoon of phone calls the chief constable received orders to let them go on parole providing they agreed not to take any part in the war – this included writing anything in German or giving money to anyone who was German. Ironically, the Germans were so grateful for the considerate treatment they received from the British police that they made a sizeable donation to charity as a mark of their thanks.

Foreign men on boats were a particular problem as they often didn't realise they had to register, particularly if they were not leaving the boat. The first prosecutions under the Aliens Restriction Act of 1914 were heard in court on 11 August 1914, when two men were charged with failing to register as aliens and another with leaving his registered address without notifying the authorities. One man was bound over, but the other two were held on remand pending further enquiries. Another German, Andrew Hochheim, a tailor described as a 'white haired old man aged 56' living at the Church Army Home was remanded at Middlesbrough. Although he said he was born in Mulhausen, he said he had lived in England since 1883.

Two German sailors charged on 17 August 1914, not realising the need to register, had been advised to remain on board their Danish vessel and just give no trouble. The men were bound over on the surety of the captain.

Many other cases of this kind occurred during the autumn of 1914, with the police carefully checking all shipping registers. The patience of the authorities soon began to wear thin. Two more men who were fined on 13 August for not registering, were told that if they did not comply they would be sent to prison for six months.

By 22 August 1914, over 400 German and Austrian subjects had been registered. In September, under the Aliens Registration Act and Order 1914, Middlesbrough was declared a prohibited area, meaning that no alien enemy could continue to live in the town without special permission from the chief constable and that every alien, whether enemy or not, must be registered.

Aliens who, through ten years residency lawfully qualified for jury service, were struck off the lists. From 12 October 1914, the Aliens Restriction Order forbade aliens from having any other surname other than the one they had at the beginning of the war. Landladies were told that if they had any lodgers who were aliens they had to report them to the authorities. By the end of October, aliens were being rounded up wholesale and the *North-Eastern Daily Gazette* announced that the last twenty Germans and Austrians had been taken into custody, thus 'clearing the town of aliens'.

Disturbing the Peace

With the BEF landing in France on 7 August 1914 and then suffering casualties at Mons two weeks later, anti-German feelings, fuelled by propaganda, developed quickly in Middlesbrough. Hostile nationalistic fervour easily gained a foothold in a town where a male dominated society, with its collective comradeship, proved an easy germinating ground for pro-war feelings and xenophobic behaviour. It was only a matter of time before this spilled over into the streets, and consequently a number of unpleasant disturbances took place in Middlesbrough featuring attacks on those termed as 'enemy aliens'.

The first report of an unprovoked attack was on 12 August 1914, when an Italian ice cream vendor in Bridge Street was beaten by several youths from one of the local works.

The situation worsened when the long-awaited first official casualty lists for the British Expeditionary Force were made public on Thursday, 3 September – others followed on 4, 8 and 10 September. The lists filled whole columns in the *North-Eastern Daily Gazette* and, along with news of HMS *Pathfinder* being sunk by a U-boat off the coast of St Abb's Head, Berwickshire, on Saturday 5 September, with the loss of 259 men, anti-German feeling increased rapidly.

As ever, on Friday, 4 September 1914, the platforms and the area around the station were congested as large numbers of family and friends waved an emotional goodbye. The packed troop trains left Middlesbrough most evenings at 10.48 p.m., carrying men from the town in response to Kitchener's call. After the train departed, emotions enhanced by an evening drinking, were running very high. Despite the authorities allowing a great deal of license, a large unruly crowd of mainly women and youths made their way from the station area to gather in Cannon Street opposite the Cannon Hotel. The report of Chief Constable Henry Riches later described how emotions ran over and the crowd attacked the shop of Peter Krauss, a locksmith who traded in Cannon Street.

Krauss, who lived at the premises with his German wife, Lizette, and their four grown up sons, was born in Germany but had come to England in 1863, as a 13-year-old boy, with his father who was now a naturalised British subject. This was a volatile situation; a window in the Cannon Hotel was broken, and considerable damage was caused by stone-throwing to the Off Beer House opposite the locksmith's shop. As the crowd, described as very hostile, began to gain the upper hand, police dealing with the situation had to send an urgent telephone message to the central police station for reinforcements.

Eventually cleared from Cannon Street, the rowdy crowd then headed for nearby Newport Road, where they attacked the shop of pork butcher Henry Schumm. Like Krauss, Schumm was also a naturalised British subject as was his father before him, though both had been born in Germany. The sense of riot continued as the crowd, having been dispersed by the police moved on to the town's main thoroughfare, Linthorpe Road, where they attacked another shop belonging to Schumm. These scenes continued into the night until nearly 4 a.m., when the crowd eventually broke up. They were an outward sign of just how high feelings were running as the reality of the war came to Middlesbrough. Ironically, the Schumm family had the previous week featured in the list of those from Middlesbrough giving money to the Prince of Wales National Relief Fund, having donated five guineas (£5.25).

This was not an isolated incident. More violent scenes occurred the following evening, Saturday, 5 September 1914. Police reports noted worryingly that many of the crowd involved were ordinary law-abiding citizens who seemed determined to obstruct the police from doing their duty. In North Ormesby at 10.30 p.m., over 2,000 people gathered in Smeaton Street outside another butcher's shop owned by a German. Only a strong police presence kept the crowd in check. Simultaneously, a crowd had gathered again in central Middlesbrough, starting in Cannon Street before spreading to Newport Road and then to Parliament Road. There they attacked the shop of 29-year-old William Schumm, born in Middlesbrough. The attack was well planned as the crowd arrived with sticks, broom handles and lead weights, singing 'It's a Long Way to Tipperary'. Every window was smashed, with the single policeman on duty helplessly unable to prevent the damage. Once again, much damage was done before the crowd finally dispersed at 3 a.m. At times almost the whole of the available police force was out on the streets in an attempt to prevent further trouble, using local taxis to move around the town.

On the Sunday, for a third successive night, the police were out on the streets, this time accompanied by two members of the Town Council, Alderman Alfred Mattison and Councillor Turner. Sporadic disturbances continued throughout September with the ringleaders, one of whom was a woman, either fined or sentenced to hard labour. In an attempt to quell the uprisings, the departure time of the troop trains leaving Middlesbrough each evening was switched to 6.04 p.m. Henry Riches reported that this was successful, as the 'congestion was ... much relieved'.

Although these were the most serious disturbances during the war, they were not the only incidents. On 17 May 1915, ten days after the sinking of RMS *Lusitania*, there were again attacks made, in Newport Road, on the business premises of citizens with a German name, although the victims had been born in Middlesbrough. There was always increased tension when other wartime events were reported, often leaving the mayor having to call for restraint among people in the town.

It's so Bloomin' Dark

In October 1914, in response to an instruction from the Home Office, it was decided to light only one half of the town's streetlights. Shopkeepers were told to pull their sun blinds down when shop lamps were lit to restrict lights visible from either the sea or the air. By February 1915, under DORA (Defence of the Realm Act), came further restrictions with all inside and outside lights of shop windows to be extinguished by 6.30 p.m. This brought considerable complaints from traders.

Other restrictions included: the extinguishing of 50 per cent of the lighting in side streets from 5 p.m. and 75 per cent in main roads; tram cars had to be curtained inside with no lights showing; and all street lights to be extinguished after 9.30 p.m. In April 1915, the order was modified again to take effect from one hour after sunset to one hour before sunrise.

Even car headlights were subject to heavy restrictions, and for safety perambulators had to carry a light after dark. This proved extremely difficult for those women who had to take their children with them when they left the house at night, especially as lamps were not easily accessible. Eventually an amendment was issued that prams on the footpath or crossing the street from one path to another need not be lit.

A 'Daylight Saving' scheme was brought in during 1916, and the first day of British Summer Time (BST) was Sunday, 21 May 1916. The *North-Eastern Daily Gazette* carried full instructions on how to put the clocks forward and that BST would end on 30 September 1916. The jeweller R. Richardson, who had a shop on Linthorpe Road, had the task of changing over 500 clocks in municipal offices, institutions, works and residences. He said he would begin the evening before, to try to complete this task on time.

THE BANK OF ENGLAND AND THE WAR

The whole question of business is underpinned by the economy, managed and regulated by government and the Bank of England. In the few days before war began, a series of high-level consultations took place between the Bank of England, the clearing bankers and the Treasury.

In the previous five days, the 'unprecedented sum' of over £27 million had been advanced, and there were fears the bank, with its reserves down to £9.967 million, might collapse. The bank rate went up to 10 per cent, causing great alarm amongst the public.

Other moves followed on Sunday 2 August: a moratorium was declared (meaning no debts could be recovered by law until a date was fixed) and the bank holiday was extended by three days. The moratorium continued (with monthly renewals) until 4 November, giving some time for the accepting houses to recover.

When the Middlesbrough County Court met on 10 August, His Honour Judge Templer would not listen to any summons for debts before 28 October – much to the relief of the large number of debtors in court!

The extra bank holiday was an inconvenience, with individuals and trade unable to obtain cash, posing a particular problem for those in shipping, as the necessary cash payments could not be made to members of the crew and other personnel. This led to delays in some ships at Middlesbrough loading up their cargo. When the banks did reopen on Friday 7 August, the public discovered that they would no longer be paid in gold, but in a new legal tender of Treasury notes (£1 notes in black, 10s notes in red).

Prominent notices were displayed in the *North-Eastern Daily Gazette* to inform and reassure the public. There seemed to be few problems with the public accepting the new notes, until they began to appear in wage packets, at which point a further newspaper campaign ran to reassure the public that postal orders (used by some employers) and paper money still held the same value as a gold coin. However, to confuse matters, the £1 notes issued in August 1914 were replaced in late October with the new note being described as 'far handsomer' than the crude design of the old one.

*Middlesbrough Exchange was the financial heart of
the town's iron and steel industry. (Courtesy of Teesside Archives)*

4

KEEP THE HOME FIRES BURNING

Stranded Abroad

Keeping the people of Middlesbrough safe during the First World War was understandably a key priority. However, this should not deflect from the many other events that went on during the war as the town struggled through these difficult years.

When war began, some of the most challenging circumstances were those facing people from Middlesbrough who had been travelling in Europe. Although there are no records of any tourists failing to return, there were some interesting exploits. An unnamed young woman from Middlesbrough travelled to Paris to attend an Esperanto Congress on Saturday 1 August. When she arrived she found herself confined to St Lazare Station. Anticipating a problem, she took events into her own hands and decided to return immediately. Many other people were also trying to leave and this meant a very physical struggle for a place hidden in the luggage van of a train leaving for Dieppe. At the Channel port she faced another free-for-all to get on an overcrowded boat to England where, to her great relief, she arrived on Monday morning. She described the situation in Paris as 'chaotic'.

Another traveller who expressed 'great relief' on arriving back at Middlesbrough on Wednesday 5 August, was a gentleman who was travelling in Holland and Belgium. During his return he had endured difficult and extensive searches of his luggage, when

German soldiers on the Belgian frontier had confronted him. The town clerk of Middlesbrough, Preston Kitchen, was also in Belgium touring with his wife. Returning from Knocke-sur-Mer, a resort north of Blankenberge on the Belgian coast, they met with considerable delays and, arriving back in Middlesbrough, Kitchen described it as a 'rather trying experience'.

Many other people travelling further afield in Austria or Switzerland also found their return delayed. William Pattison of Middlesbrough and his German wife, Marta, found themselves separated for a time on the outbreak of war. Having married in 1910 in Frankfurt, they had returned to live in Middlesbrough. When war began Marta was visiting Germany with their two daughters, and expected William to join her in August. War prevented him from making the journey and, unable to return, Marta was seemingly stranded in Germany. It wasn't until October 1914 that the family was finally reunited.

Two other ladies from Middlesbrough were visiting a town on the Franco–German border on the day war began. Unable to leave for several days, they witnessed the mobilisation of German troops. Their journey home included hitching a ride in a cattle truck before sailing to Folkestone. They spoke well of the Germans, but added that the people in Germany couldn't begin to understand why Britain had declared war against them.

One of the most dramatic stories concerned Mrs Mary Roberts, aged 37, whose husband, Joseph, was the manager at the town's Corporation Hotel. Mary had sailed, with her 13-year-old son, on the Norwegian steamship, the SS *Skala*, for the Russian port of Riga. Joseph, having had a telegraph from Mary on her arrival saying she would write, became very worried when he heard nothing more, especially as the nearby town of Libau was reported as being shelled by the Germans. Even the shipping agents were unable to find any trace of the ship. On her eventual return in mid-August she had quite a tale to tell. When the captain of the *Skala* realised his ship would be prohibited from leaving the port he had arrived at the house where Mary was staying, just before midnight one evening, to say he was sailing from Riga at 6 a.m. the next morning. To help Mary and her son make their escape, he signed them on as a stewardess and a ship's boy. It was a difficult voyage through the Baltic Sea – they were turned back once and there was the ever-present danger of mines. When a German battleship forced the *Skala* to stop for investigation, the wily captain told Mrs Roberts to disguise herself as a peasant woman, by using coal dust to cover her face. Despite the close scrutiny of German officers who boarded the ship, it worked! Eventually they reached Arandal in Norway, from where they travelled overland to Bergen to take the passenger steamer to Newcastle, where they arrived much relieved.

We're All in this Together

As the initial exhilaration gave way to more serious deliberations, the implications of being at war became more apparent. Middlesbrough Borough Council threw all its resources into maintaining the morale of the people, so on the first Sunday of the war, in a show of civic strength, the mayor and members of the council attended a special church service at St Hilda's Church in the old town. After the congregation had sung 'Oh, God our help in ages past', Canon William Thomas Lawson of North Ormesby, said in his sermon that, 'the outbreak of war was a supreme crisis, but that Britain had entered it as a moral duty and moreover, that war was not with the German people, but with German statesmanship'.

It was difficult not to be affected in some way by the war in those first few days and weeks. Economic consequences were widespread. The summer tourist trade was ruined, and local seaside resorts badly hit by loss of business. August was their peak season, but the commandeering of trains by the military greatly reduced the number of people travelling to resorts. Even when NER resumed some normal summer excursions in mid-August there was still a reluctance to travel, as trains were still liable to be cancelled at the last minute. Saltburn was said to be very quiet, with hardly any visitors. Many bookings had been cancelled, whilst many of those who were on holiday were packing up and returning home. There was even an appeal in

Middlesbrough for owners of horses and carts to volunteer to take local poor children to the seaside, as they were being deprived of their much loved annual visit to the coast.

Many events were cancelled. Stokesley Agricultural Show was abandoned for the first time in its fifty year history in mid-August, causing major disappointment, as the funfair in the town was also lost. The agricultural show at Thorpe Thewles was called off, along with events at Danby (20 August), Hinderwell (26 August) and the Whitby Regatta, scheduled for 24 August. For those agricultural shows that went ahead, including those at Liverton Mines and Great Ayton, attendances were considerably lower than normal.

Even when the immediate panic subsided and normality seemed to be returning, tourist numbers were reported as being very low. It was late August before Redcar reported that visitors were returning despite the 'absurd rumours about the beaches being barricaded and the promenades being shut off'. Coastal towns *were* heavily guarded, however, and this did bring awkward confrontations between tourists and the military. Despite visitors being alerted to the dangers of evening walks along beaches patrolled by military forces, one visitor who ignored the warning to take their usual walk, ran off with fright when challenged by a soldier. They were fortunate that the guard did not take more serious action.

Another sign of normality returning was the resumption, on the evening of 15 August, of the Tyne and Tees Shipping Company's passenger service between London and Stockton and Middlesbrough. The SS *Buccaneer* left London for the Tees whilst the SS *Claudia* left Middlesbrough for London. Two years later at 8.40 a.m. on Sunday 30 July 1916, the SS *Claudia*, loaded with general cargo and steel, was sunk by a mine from the German submarine *UC-1*, 8.5 miles south-east from Lowestoft, on a voyage from Middlesbrough to London. The captain, C.W. Jordan, and nineteen members of the crew were saved, but unfortunately three members of the crew, all from Middlesbrough, were killed. No passengers were on board. This sinking was felt with much regret in the town, as the steamship was well known, having transported many local passengers between Middlesbrough and London since it was built in 1897.

The SS Claudia, *operated by the Tyne and Tees Shipping Company on the passenger service between the Tees and London, was sunk near Lowestoft on 30 July 1916 when it hit a mine, killing three Middlesbrough men. (Courtesy of Shipwrecks UK)*

One of the most urgent tasks was preparing for the arrival of the wounded from Belgium and France. When the war began many offers of accommodation were received, ranging from large country houses to schools and smaller private houses. Suitable properties were then converted into hospital units, each being linked to a regional military hospital. These improvised hospitals received a grant from the War Office of 3*s* (15p) per day for each patient they received, and were expected to raise additional funds themselves. Staffing included a commandant with overall responsibility, except for medical and nursing services, a quartermaster responsible for matters concerning provisions, a matron who directed the trained nursing staff (some qualified nurses were employed), members of the local Voluntary Aid Detachment and a number of paid staff who did clerical, kitchen and various maintenance tasks.

Like many other towns, Middlesbrough, which was part of the British Red Cross, North Riding of Yorkshire branch, had only a short time to prepare to cope with the fallout of war. However, with many offers of help it was announced by the mayor within the first week of war, that preparations had been made for up to

300 wounded men, with motor vehicles available to take them to hospitals. Beds were prepared in Marton Road School, but with the new term approaching they were moved to the Friends Meeting House, and then to a house in Southfield Road. There were also beds on the up-platform and the waiting room at Middlesbrough Station. A request from the St John Ambulance Association, for volunteer ambulance men to attend a meeting at 7 p.m. on 14 August at the Town Hall, resulted in 130 men coming forward, as well as a number of stretchers being offered for use.

The Middlesbrough Liberal Association, with Mrs Penry Williams in the chair, offered to help the mayor to obtain clothing for the wounded and organise classes in emergency nursing. When a letter to the *North-Eastern Daily Gazette* suggested that children could make pillows for the wounded by collecting old material, cutting it up and stuffing calico cases, Jones' Sewing Machine Co. Ltd announced that they would lend an unlimited number of machines for the sewing effort. The pillows were then delivered to the 'Guild of Help' at the Town Hall. The mayor even issued a circular requesting that those who grew grapes in their greenhouse reserve as many as they could spare for the wounded soldiers when they arrive.

Local hospitals were a crucial part of the scheme, and were keen to help. At North Ormesby Hospital special arrangements had been made, with a good supply of surgical requisites bought in, and the hospital played its part in receiving wounded men throughout the war. At the North Riding Infirmary, plans agreed several years previously were initiated within a week of war breaking out; this meant sixty beds were made available without disruption to the main running of the hospital. When only a small number of military cases (twelve men – who had all been wounded whilst training in this country) had arrived by November 1914, this was reduced to one large ward capable of accommodating twenty adults, retained in case of emergency need. Bolckow and Vaughan announced, on 10 August, that the firm's hospitals at Eston and Cleveland House, South Bank, were being offered to the Admiralty for the reception of wounded men and the White House at Coatham for men convalescing.

Elsewhere, sixteen beds provided in a yard at Smith's Dock, South Bank, were placed at the disposal of the commanding officers at the South Gare and Hartlepool, where the 5th Durham Light Infantry were guarding the entrance to the Tees. With the August race meeting abandoned, the buildings at Redcar racecourse were also placed at the disposal of the war authorities for use as a hospital if the coast was invaded.

A British Red Cross VAD Hospital was established at the Holgate Workhouse, Middlesbrough, by 'special request of the Deputy Director Medical Services (DDMS), Northern Command'. Using the 'female infirm blocks' the hospital, which opened on 25 October 1917, was used for 'the treatment of sick troops from the Tees Garrison stationed in the district and proved invaluable to the large number of men who received treatment during the two years it was open'. There were fifty-one beds, and a total of 577 patients were treated at a cost of 5s 1d (26p) per day.

Table 1 gives details of some British Red Cross hospitals in the Middlesbrough area during the war period. Note that the 'household staff' is recorded as helping out at one hospital. In private houses, household rooms became medical wards, and gardens became places of convalescence. Many patients said they preferred the more 'homely' atmosphere and less strict routine compared with a military hospital. With a total of 8,891 men cared for and, in most cases nursed back to health, the work of these hospitals was vital.

Occupational therapy at the British Red Cross hospital Crathorne Hall in 1915. (Courtesy of The Lord Crathorne)

Table 1: British Red Cross Hospitals: Middlesbrough District 1914–19

Location	Date Opened	Date Closed	No. of Beds	Total Patients Treated	Affiliated to	Commandant i/c	Red Cross Unit
The Manor House Hospital, Stokesley. (Mrs L. Gjers)	28 October 1914	18 January 1919	60	801	East Leeds War Hospital	Mrs L. Gjers	Yorks/42
Ayton Firs' Hospital, Great Ayton. (Mr & Mrs Kitching*)	10 December 1914	11 November 1915	20	50	Military Hospital, York	Mrs Kitching	Trained Nurses & Household Staff
Crathorne Hall Hospital, Crathorne, nr. Yarm. (J.L. Dugdale*)	13 November 1914	9 July 1917	24	423	War Hospital, Newcastle	Mrs J.L. Dugdale	Yorks/24 & Trained Nurses
Rounton Red Cross Aux. Hospital, Rounton. (Sir Hugh Bell)	25 November 1914	3 January 1919	37	387	Military Hospital, York	Lady F. Bell	Yorks/44 & Trained Nurses
Red Cross Hospital, Holgate, Middlesbrough. (M'boro Board of Guardians)	1 October 1917	30 April 1919	51	577	Newcastle General	Mrs May Hedley	Yorks/32 & Trained Nurses
Hemlington Aux. Hospital, Middlesbrough.	17 September 1914	8 August 1918	150	3,345	War Hospital, Newcastle	Dr Longbotham/ Dr Ellis	Yorks/29 & Trained Nurses
Red Barns Hospital, Redcar ** (Sir Hugh Bell)	9 January 1915	30 April 1919	90	1,345	East Leeds War Hospital	Mrs C. Pease	Yorks/8 & Trained Nurses
Giffden' Red Cross Hospital, Saltburn, (est. by Miss Robertson)	23 December 1914	16 August 1919	50	1152	East Leeds War Hospital	A.J. Longley	Yorks/76 & Trained Nurses
Chaloner Hall Hospital, Guisborough. (Lord & Lady Guisborough)	13 December 1915	31 March 1917	20	220	Military Hospital, York	Lady Holden of Aston	Yorks/26 & Trained Nurses
Barton Hall' Hospital, Skelton	1 April 1915	19 January 1919	36	480	East Leeds War Hospital	E.J. Burnett	Yorks/20

* Indicates all expenses incurred, including the building, paid for by owners.
** Although not in the list, Kirkleatham Hall was also used as an auxiliary hospital.

Hemlington Hospital

The largest recipient of wounded men in the Middlesbrough area was Hemlington Hospital. Following a smallpox epidemic in 1898, Middlesbrough Borough Council had decided they needed another isolation unit and purchased the 65-acre site at Belle Vue Farm, Hemlington, for £3,000 in 1900. Opening in March 1905, Hemlington Hospital consisted of a number of brick linked corrugated iron, single storey, double ward pavilions with a capacity for 190 patients and administration buildings, including quarters for up to thirty-five resident staff. In 1914 the hospital mainly housed patients with TB. Between 17 September 1914 and 8 August 1918, Hemlington Hospital acted as an auxiliary to the 1st Northern General Hospital in Newcastle, admitting 3,345 men of which only three died during that time – though this suggests that men with less serious injuries were sent there.

The problems of running Hemlington typify some of the challenges faced by British Red Cross auxiliary hospitals during the war. These included the financial burden, staffing, general maintenance, looking after the men themselves and last but not least, the out-of-the-way location of the site. The latter proved to be very significant at Hemlington, a remote establishment, reached from a lonely country lane only by means of a single track.

Coping with casualties at the Front was a difficult task for the army. A field ambulance unit provided initial care, before the wounded were removed to a casualty clearing station, sometimes several miles behind the front line. The next stage was a base hospital in France, or being sent back to the United Kingdom for further treatment or convalescence.

Having decided in the first week of war to place Hemlington Hospital at the disposal of the British Red Cross Society, the process to get it ready was already ongoing when the mayor announced the decision at a special council meeting on 28 August. As well as the 150 beds at Hemlington Hospital, and twenty beds at the Cleveland Asylum being made available, Middlesbrough's Floating Hospital had also been requisitioned for Red Cross work. The mayor also announced that Sir Willans Nussey, on behalf of the British Red Cross, had inspected and approved the facilities. The Middlesbrough Hospital and Clothing Fund, which began work in the first week of the war, announced that they were ready to equip twenty of the beds at Hemlington Hospital. The TB patients had been returned to their homes, or sent to West Lane Sanatorium when Hemlington Hospital closed to TB patients on 7 August 1914 – a move which was not without its critics. Replying to these, the authorities stated at a meeting, on 16 September 1914, that patients had not been disadvantaged by the move and that the percentage of deaths had, in fact, decreased.

HEMLINGTON ISOLATION HOSPITAL—ADMINISTRATIVE BUILDINGS.

HEMLINGTON ISOLATION HOSPITAL—LAUNDRY, DISINFECTOR, AND STORES.

The administrative buildings, laundry and stores at Hemlington Hospital. (Courtesy of Teesside Archives)

A typical ward as used at Hemlington Hospital for wounded soldiers. (Courtesy of Teesside Archives)

Dr Charles Vincent Dingle, the medical officer of health for Middlesbrough, undertook responsibility for staffing. Under his leadership, a rota was compiled of volunteer local doctors to treat patients. Many women volunteered to start training for their roles as nursing staff. The Voluntary Aid Detachment, British Red Cross Society (No 29 Yorks), a men's detachment, were assigned to Hemlington with Drs Longbotham and Body in charge. The 29th Yorks, originally formed on 11 April 1914 to deal with industrial emergencies rather than war casualties, coped commendably throughout the war, in duties as ambulance men, and at their posts during Zeppelin 'air-raids'. Initially there were no shortages of volunteer nursing staff, 'middle-class ladies willing to do their bit' as they have sometimes been unfairly labelled. Although some only served a short time, generally the volunteers provided an invaluable service and a valuable contribution to wartime medical care.

The town clerk of Middlesbrough, Preston Kitchen, was advised on Thursday, 17 September 1914, that the first group of seventy-two men being transferred from Newcastle would arrive on the 4.47 p.m. train. The carriages were gently shunted alongside the southern platform, where the mayor waited to greet them. He had ordered refreshments, and Dr Dingle had asked the young women from the sanatorium to serve coffee and food when the men had left the train. Many other helpers came eagerly forward and handed round cigarettes. Although some soldiers were obviously in pain, they were reported as 'smiling cheerfully and bearing up'. Most men could walk, but some were carried on stretchers to the fleet of 'motorcars and motor buses' waiting to take them to Hemlington. Crowds continually cheered the convoy as it passed through the streets of Middlesbrough.

This first group of men had all sustained their injuries in this country, and they had been moved from Newcastle to vacate beds which were needed for wounded men being sent from France. Many of the subsequent arrivals at Hemlington, however, had been wounded at the Front.

The next batch of arrivals on Monday, 28 September, were a group of forty-three soldiers, many of whom had been wounded at Mons, and this certainly brought a sense of the bloody horror of war. When they arrived at Middlesbrough Station their appearance silenced the waiting crowd, though they recovered their voices to cheer as they boarded the waiting ambulances. The men, from the Scottish Fusiliers, the 3rd Coldstream Guards, the 5th Dragoon Guards, the Royal Artillery and the 1st Duke of Cornwall's Light Infantry, had been in the thick of the fighting at both Mons and the Marne. Their stirring tales – including the atrocities carried out by the Germans, were reported in papers across the country. Newspapers as far north as Aberdeen carried their story due to Scottish regiments being involved.

Two days later, yet another batch of men arrived – most were suffering from leg wounds sustained from fighting at the Front. They were taken to Hemlington Hospital on a large motorbus provided by the Imperial Tramway Company.

The following week, on Monday, 5 October, thirty more wounded arrived (the third group in a week) at the northern platform of Middlesbrough Station. Some wore bandages around their head and face, but most had shrapnel wounds to the legs – one soldier proudly carried in his hand the actual shrapnel that had hit him. With a now familiar routine, organisers at the station buffet gave refreshments to the men on their arrival, before the soldiers walked into the station yard to board the cars and motorbus waiting to go to Hemlington Hospital. Among the cheering crowds were three local survivors from HMS *Hogue*, one of three ships sunk by German U-boats on 22 September, who were reported as cheering louder than anyone else. The procession of vehicles was a poignant sight in the fading afternoon light as it wove its way through the gaslit streets of the town. Having travelled along Acklam Road, the convoy reached open countryside where it passed Blue Bell Farm, then Viewley Hill, before slowing down at the crossroads in Hemlington, a small hamlet of a few houses. Local people stood on the corner and cheered as the convoy turned into the narrow lane. A few hundred yards later the vehicles slowed again as they turned into the entrance to the hospital site. A long, winding tree-lined dirt track full of potholes had to be navigated in the dark before they arrived at the brightly lit single storey hospital buildings. For some, who were a long way from their family, these out-of-the-way corrugated iron buildings nearly 6 miles from town, would be home in the weeks to come.

Thank You, Nurse

First reports indicated that the men were reasonably happy with conditions at Hemlington, and very appreciative of the attention from the matron, Miss Rosina Webb, and her staff. However, the isolation of the hospital was clearly an issue from the beginning; many men, more used to the bright lights of towns and cities, soon found the view over the fields to Newby and Hemlington Grange tedious, and even oppressive. As their health improved they wanted, metaphorically or literally, to escape the confines of the wards and experience life outside the hospital.

During the early days of the war the people of Middlesbrough were enthusiastic to help the men, but as the realities of war made life more of a struggle for ordinary people, the offers of help became less frequent. Initial donations of books and magazines were so numerous that the matron was forced to suggest that notepaper and envelopes would be a welcome alternative.

The men, on the other hand, preferred donations of cigarettes and tobacco. These were always in demand, as supplying the 100 patients with a modest five cigarettes each day required 500 cigarettes per day – an overall daily outlay of

7s 1d (35p) – the equivalent of the War Office daily allowance for two men! The military authorities, through the mayor, appealed for daily donations of these items. Several business establishments, including the Middlesbrough wine merchant, Winterschladen's Co. Ltd, displayed special boxes for customers to put donations in. Ironically founded by a German, Joseph Winterschladen, the company donated 800 cigarettes in response to the mayor's appeal and continued to do so on a regular basis.

On Monday, 28 September, a dispatch rider returned from taking newspapers to Hemlington Hospital to report that the soldiers were so short of tobacco and cigarettes that he was to personally organise donations, preferably of Woodbines and twist tobacco. The daily visit of the young dispatch rider from Middlesbrough, whose motorcycle was so noisy the men could hear him coming, relieved the feeling of restlessness. The dispatch rider became one of their best friends as he arrived laden with newspapers and items ranging from bootlaces to postage stamps, toiletries to matches. The latest *North-Eastern Daily Gazette* was always eagerly awaited, as everyone wanted to know the latest football results and news of the war. On his way back he usually took a batch of letters to be posted in town.

The men enjoyed some fraternisation with the town and the Middlesbrough public, when occasionally they attended public events. These included free tickets to visit one of the town's theatres – sometimes the transport would be paid for too – or a visit to Ayresome Park to watch Middlesbrough Football Club (League football continued until the end of the 1914/15 season). The soldiers occasionally got the opportunity to repay the hospitality shown to them and a small group of wounded men from the hospital took part in the military procession through the town that preceded the large recruitment meeting at the Town Hall on 11 November 1914. Three days earlier, one patient, Gunner Geoffrey Bassier appeared in a concert for the Prince of Wales National Relief Fund, singing a selection of patriotic songs at the Empire Theatre in Middlesbrough. It is not difficult to imagine the applause, and the rousing effect on the audience the appearance of these men brought to these events.

Unfortunately, the hospitality proved too much on some occasions. One young 19-year-old soldier, who had been given a ticket to see the football match at Middlesbrough, was bought so many drinks by the thankful public that he ended up in court charged with being drunk and disorderly and resisting the police. The judiciary heard he had fought in the Battles of the Marne and the Aisne, and had shown good character whilst at Hemlington, so were lenient in fining him 7s 6d (35p).

Alf Smith, Organiser Extraordinaire

Evenings were the worst time for the men. Many evenings were spent playing cards, and a miniature billiard table and a piano were also well used. Middlesbrough's famous swimmer, Jack Hatfield, even sent the soldiers a football. During that first autumn a regular supply of flowers and tomatoes were sent from people's gardens to Hemlington Hospital, led by the mayoress, who lived at Woodside, The Avenue, in Linthorpe. These were welcomed not just by the men, but also by the authorities who were always happy to reduce costs.

There were many concerts held at Hemlington Hospital for the men – usually a group of local artistes would come in and perform for a couple of hours. A key figure in the organisation of this was Middlesbrough resident, Alf Smith. He gave a huge amount of time to organising, arranging and even appearing in the concerts. When Henderson's Ltd, of Newcastle, supplied an evening of cinematograph pictures on 21 October 1914, and a musician was needed to play the accompanying piano music to the silent film, Alf Smith stepped in.

A written description of an evening concert, which took place on 21 October 1916, survives. It was a special night, as a presentation took place to mark Alf Smith's two years as concert organiser. The Middlesbrough Phoenix Club, hosts for the evening, arrived with lots of 'cigarettes, tobacco and matches and other things dear to the heart of Tommy Atkins' for the 'hospital boys in blue'. Following the usual introduction on

Alf Smith, 1916. (Courtesy of the Evening Gazette, *Middlesbrough)*

a makeshift stage, the evening was one of rapturous applause and joyous laughter with comics, saucy songs and opera. When the interval came, Sergeant Annesley of the Liverpool Scottish stepped forward. Everyone but Alf knew what was happening. Annesley began his warm tribute to Alf, who 'for two years had provided weekly concerts for the wounded at Hemlington Hospital … the maimed, bandaged soldiers, the flotsam tossed up by the merciless tide of war, had no truer friend than Alf Smith'. As he received his gift of a smoker's cabinet and case of pipes, subscribed for by the wounded soldiers, matron and staff, Smith was, for once, speechless as he listened to the loud applause and cheering. When he did eventually reply, he said he had done it all out of sense of duty.

There were occasional distinguished guests eager to be seen visiting the men. Penry Williams spent a cheerful evening there talking to the men, before he went to join his regiment. On 13 October the Archbishop of York, Dr Cosmo Lang, visited, and spent a very informal hour shaking the hands of all the men and chatting about the war. The news was not good, as news of the fall of Antwerp had just been received.

The glamorous French artiste and singer, Liane D'Eve, who was appearing at the Empire in Middlesbrough for a week, caused quite a stir when she took along the whole theatre company, travelling in a cavalcade of motor cars to visit the wounded at Hemlington Hospital. They even gave an impromptu concert and sang for the troops during the visit. This must have been a memorable evening for the men, who surely would have been very moved at the visit of this caval-cade to their hospital wards.

Who'd be a VAD?

As the first winter approached, over 100 men from many different units, including the Coldstream Guards, Dragoon Guards, the Durham's, Worcester's, Northumberland Fusiliers and Cornwall Light Infantry, were being cared for at the hospital.

Managing the hospital could be difficult. Shortly after a group of Belgian soldiers who couldn't speak any English arrived, there were rumours of trouble between the British soldiers and the Belgians and this resulted in one of the Belgian soldiers making a public denial of anything going on. In a letter to the *North-Eastern Daily Gazette* on 27 November, G. Sloighmuylder, Regiment des Grenadiers, a patient at the hospital, said that this was 'a scandalous lie [and] there wasn't a body of men more agreeable. I hope the Middlesbrough public take this piffle for what it is worth.'

Other problems also feature in the hospital records. There were complaints from neighbouring farms about sanitation and refuse from the hospital polluting their land. When six of the volunteer nurses living on site asked to keep a dog for security, they were told this wasn't allowed. They were told, however, that a guard dog would be bought for the hand at the farm, but he would have sole charge. When one nurse ignored this and bought her own dog, she was discovered when the dog began to worry the sheep of local farms.

A VAD certificate issued by the British Red Cross in 1916. (Courtesy of the Dorman Museum)

Even the matron, Rosina Webb, was sanctioned when Robert Walshaw of neighbouring Larchfield Farm complained that her chickens had damaged his crops. The matron was warned to 'keep her poultry under proper control'.

Another nurse was warned that the hospital authorities did not approve of her inviting her relatives to stay in the residential quarters of the hospital.

In June 1915 there were allegations in the *North-Eastern Daily Gazette* about the 'poor quality food' being served to the men. A deputation from the council discussed this with the men and some of the staff, but other than the assertion that they were served 'bully beef' for breakfast five mornings in a row it seemed to be without foundation. Matron Webb argued that it had only been three mornings in a row, and that this was due to supplies of bacon which had not arrived at the hospital. One result of this inquiry was that more cups and saucers were ordered (before then men had to have their cups of tea in 'shifts'), tablecloths were supplied and the provision of a dining room or marquee considered, as the hospital had originally been intended for bed patients only.

Out of Town

The major concern, though, was the isolated location. This meant that transport had always to be available to transport local doctors on the rota to the hospital, or to take nursing staff to town. The Corporation had a motor vehicle based at Hemlington Hospital, but running this proved expensive with the sheer number of journeys as well as the poor state of the roads resulting in lots of expensive repairs. Vehicle problems worsened, until on 5 November 1915 it was announced that the offer, from Mr Neasham of Middlesbrough, of a new Ford (1916 model) for £135 (with £3 delivery costs) less £50 allowed for the old car was to be accepted. The new vehicle would be kept strictly under the control of a driver recently appointed at a salary of 25s (£1.25) a week.

The poorly maintained country roads made it difficult for both cars and public transport when patients were brought to the hospital. An idea to convert the car, originally fitted with a 'Touring Body', into an ambulance to make transporting stretcher cases easier, was rejected.

A letter from Mr Freshwater, the manager of Imperial Tramways Company Limited, stated they were refusing to allow their motor bus to go up to the hospital until the track from the road was 'put in proper order'. The huge gatepost at the start of the track was also difficult, causing the bus problems when it tried to negotiate the corner entering into the lane. When a report from the borough engineer stated that repairs would cost £30–£50, the council decided to inform the War Office that they should make other arrangements for transporting patients between Hemlington Hospital and Middlesbrough Station. Ultimately, a rise in the daily allowance covered this expense.

Staffing was also a problem. When Dr Dingle, the medical officer of health for Middlesbrough, complained that many volunteer nurses 'had come for a week or two and then tired of it', the chairman of the Sanatorium Sub-Committee, Alderman McLauchlan, commented, 'You see the novelty has worn off.' In March 1915, the nine voluntary nursing staff at the hospital wrote to the council to state that, having given their services free for six months they could not continue beyond the end of the month unless allowances were given for uniform and other expenses. They eventually decided to continue, probably with resentment, when it was decided soon after to advertise for three trained surgical nurses at a salary of £30 per year. This was due to the increasing need to do surgery work rather than just nursing men through their convalescence. It created a lasting bitterness.

The soldiers themselves could also be challenging. Young, inexperienced female staff had to cope with men who had seen the horrors of war, and who could prove difficult to manage when they became bored and restless. At the request of the Sanatorium Sub-Committee, the military authorities eventually sent a resident soldier, Corporal W. Duggan, to take charge of the men at the hospital.

In June 1915, May Sterry, a volunteer nurse who lived in Borough Road, Middlesbrough, died from pleurisy and exhaustion. Since she had received no money for her services, the council paid £6 10s 6d (£6.52) towards the cost of the doctor who attended her.

With staff working and living together in such isolated confines, tensions between them were never far away. In June 1915 the matron and the sister-in-charge, a volunteer nurse, resigned their posts after the driver, Robert Hoskins, made allegations of misconduct. A counter-allegation made by Matron Webb insisted that Hoskins had refused to carry out instructions issued to him. The Sanatorium Sub-Committee backed the matron, and such was the shortage of staff they increased her salary from £50 to £65 per year. Sadly, the volunteer nurse, Mona Brady, a 25-year-old girl of 'private means' from Myshall in Ireland, died in September 1916. She had requested that her salary for the period when she was ill, a sum of £10, be returned to the council but they refused to accept the cheque.

Running Hemlington Hospital was an expensive financial liability from the start. Accounts show that the cost of maintaining the hospital infrastructure, including the salaries of the twenty-two staff employed to work there, was almost £400 per month. Occasional major upgrades, such as the installation of gas lighting throughout the hospital, proved to be expensive. This needed to be done quickly and when it was completed, at the end of October 1914 by Messrs Lambert and Sons, the cost was £107 8s (£107.40).

The role of the various voluntary committees formed in Middlesbrough in the first few months of the war proved to be invaluable in the help they provided. Many of the soldiers arrived at the hospital without sufficient clothing, and were given clothing by the Mayoress' Clothing Committee. Similarly, when they left they all received a new shirt and socks.

The only financial assistance from the military authorities, a daily allowance of up to 3s (15p) towards rations for each patient, didn't cover all the costs. This made it crucial that enough patients were sent to the hospital to maintain financial stability – to 'balance the books' the hospital needed to have seventy-five patients in residence at any one time.

Table 2: *Patients at Hemlington Hospital 1914–19**

Month	1914	1915	1916	1917	1918
JAN		48	48	60	60
FEB		83	35	71	90
MAR	Not applicable	67	63	108	84
APRIL		25	103	103	106
MAY		82	70	92	118
JUNE		60	50	76	100
JULY		62	81	75	46
AUG		62	81	75	27
SEPT	99	34	74	89	Closed
OCT	94	30	Closed	89	
NOV	89	41		109	
DEC	38	35	50	107	

*The figures are taken from the monthly report submitted by the medical officer of health to the Sanatorium Committee of Middlesbrough Borough Council.

Table 2 illustrates the variations in the number of patients, and it is clear that for many months the hospital was running at a financial loss. From December 1914–April 1916, it can be noted that in only three months were the required number of patients in residence at the hospital. It is little wonder that the council were having grave doubts about the future of Hemlington Hospital as early as June 1915 – less than nine months after it had opened. When a deputation of the mayor and members of the Sanatorium Committee travelled to York to discuss this with Surgeon General Kenny, they were told that it wasn't possible to guarantee the number of men, as smaller hospitals like Hemlington were supplied from larger regional units and it was they who decided when a wounded soldier was ready to be sent to convalesce.

The situation did not improve in 1916. The hospital was still greatly understaffed – there was only one trained nurse, when four were required. A full-time doctor was also needed, employed by the hospital rather than being dependent on the voluntary services of doctors from Middlesbrough. Various attempts to recruit more staff continued to meet with little success, and the voluntary nurses already employed there continued to ask for some payment for their services. It was becoming clear that the situation couldn't continue. The hospital received an allowance of £1 1s (£1.05) per week for each patient but the average cost of food was 12s (60p) per head.

Only in April 1916 did the hospital reach its target number of seventy-five patients, and in some weeks numbers dropped to only twenty-five patients. A special meeting of the Sanatorium Committee on 17 July 1916 found that in view of the 'inconvenient situation of the Hospital, [the problems] of maintaining a vehicular service … the lack of sufficient and efficient Nurses and domestic staff, the need for a Resident Medical Practitioner and proper Male supervision', the hospital did not meet its purpose, and should be discontinued from 30 September 1916 with all paid staff given their notice. A last minute request from the War Office in September 1916 for the hospital to remain open for an extra six weeks was reluctantly agreed to, but it was made clear that a guaranteed seventy-five patients per week would be needed for any further extension of time.

A crisis point was reached in early October 1916 when Miss Rosina Webb resigned her position as matron. There were also resignations from two nurses, the cook, two laundry maids, two housemaids and another employee, named as Miss Kirkham. This left only two nurses at the hospital. The resignations were accepted and there was a frank exchange of views as the military authorities debated the hospital's future. As a result, a number of conditions for the continuation of the hospital were met. These included a guaranteed minimum quota of seventy-five patients, the appointment of a new matron, a doctor who would be specifically employed at Hemlington Hospital and also the employment of trained nursing staff. The *North-Eastern Daily Gazette* commented that:

> … The fear that, to Middlesbrough's lasting shame, Hemlington Hospital was to close its doors to the wounded soldiers, has at last been dispelled and after a brief interval for reorganisation, the institution will continue as a military hospital for the men who have suffered injury in their country's cause.

When Hemlington Hospital reopened, on 6 December 1916, the organisational infrastructure was very different. There was a new matron, Ethel Bell, who had previous experience of this type of hospital and was recommended by the military authorities in Newcastle. Doctor R.K. Howat was appointed to work at the hospital, and trained nursing staff were also employed. A full-time residential army sergeant was put in charge of the wounded soldiers whilst they were patients there.

As well as staffing having been addressed, life for the patients was reorganised and improved. Men were allowed one visit to Middlesbrough each week. There would be two concerts at the hospital every week, and patients would receive a weekly allowance of tobacco and cigarettes, as well as fresh fruit twice a week. When a very cold spring, in 1917, brought heavy snow in late March causing a lot of problems with the corrugated iron buildings and with unprotected pipes at the hospital bursting, the authorities were much more willing to help with repair costs. This improved co-operation continued until the end of the war in 1918, and with quota numbers of patients meeting their target, the financial burden for the council was considerably eased.

In June 1918 a report from the Sanatorium Sub-Committee found that £600 would be needed to repair the buildings, if they were to continue through another winter. When Major General H.S.W. Bedford, DDMS Northern Command, was notified of this, he wrote from Northern Command HQ in York that they would no longer require the use of Hemlington beyond the time when the present patients were discharged. He also officially placed on record the 'warm appreciation of the War Department … for the kindness and devotion to the patients'.

On 6 August 1918 the last patient was examined, then subsequently discharged by an army medical officer. Hemlington Hospital closed for military purposes on 8 August 1918, and it was handed back to Middlesbrough Borough Council. By this time it was in a fairly dilapidated state and repair work took three months to complete. The future of Hemlington would be subject to much discussion, but what wasn't in doubt was its important role in the war.

Poor Little Belgium

There were many deserving people and groups asking for help during the war, and many individuals responded to this. The cause of 'Poor little Belgium' particularly captured the public conscience in Middlesbrough, exemplified by the various fundraising campaigns that were held.

On 14 September 1914 the Bishop of Middlesbrough stated that all collections in the diocese the following Sunday would be given to the fund to help the Belgians. By 15 September 1914, the Belgian Relief Fund in Middlesbrough had already raised nearly £300, despite many local people suffering great distress themselves.

On Sunday, 20 September 1914, the Teesside Irish organised a demonstration at the Hippodrome in support of Great Britain and Belgium. Nearly 2,000 people turned out for this, and a collection raised £38 4s (£38.20). A series of rousing speeches eulogised the bravery of the Belgians and, with a moving reference to the destruction of Louvain, 'denounced the atrocities carried out by the Germans'. The mayor proclaimed that more than 4,000 men from Middlesbrough had gone to fight for 'liberty, humanity and civilisation'. He brought the audience to a hush when he declared a personal interest. His daughter, Ida, educated at a convent in Belgium, had received a letter from a nun confirming the German actions. The afternoon ended with a vociferous resolution of support for the Belgian people and an emotional expression of thanks from Rev. A. Gryspeert, a Belgian citizen living in Loftus and recently returned from a visit to Belgium, before a raucous rendition of the national anthems of all the allies.

Responding to the government's offer to help Belgian war refugees, the mayor called a meeting which agreed to offer to take some refugees. The Central War Refugee Committee was informed, and William Robert Meggeson, a 58-year-old estate agent from Belle Vue, Grove Hill, offered a house on the corner of Borough and Woodlands Road, known as 'Hazeldene', for the use of the Belgians. Recently renovated, it had twelve rooms, including eight bedrooms. Numerous donations of materials to furnish the property were received. The first Belgians in the area arrived in Loftus on 26 September, where the Marquess of Zetland had placed a large house at their disposal. Marske also took seven refugees, invited by the Marchioness of Zetland, including a miner from Mons who had been separated from his wife and three children in the flight from the Germans.

The first Belgians arrived in Middlesbrough on the evening of Thursday, 8 October. They were there at the private invitation of J.W. Dalton of 32 Gurney Street, but the committee wanted civic involvement. Accordingly, Preston Kitchen, town clerk, was there to officially receive Leo Henri Gilis, his wife, and two sons aged 6 and 8, on their arrival. A small crowd had gathered at the railway station and cheered the rather bemused family. Leo, who had been employed at the printing works at Louvain, had fled with his family before the advancing German troops arrived. Leaving virtually everything behind them, they had walked almost 40 miles to Antwerp, only to find the city so crowded with refugees that they were moved on to Ostend. An attempt to return to their home in Louvain was halted at Brussels by the German military. Although they hadn't witnessed the destruction of Louvain, they had seen some horrendous scenes, including a ditch full of corpses in the village of Melle between Ghent and Termonde. The family stayed with Mr Dalton for one night, before being transferred to the house prepared for the Belgians in Woodlands Road.

On the evening of Saturday, 10 October, at 7.30 p.m. twenty-one more Belgian refugees arrived at Middlesbrough Station, from London. Most came from Malines, but two had come from Brussels. It was a very moving scene as several well-dressed families, carrying parcels, bags and baskets, their children carrying teddy bears, alighted from the train. Each member of the party had a red destination label attached to the lapel of their coat or jacket. The group included an accountant, a head clerk in a stockbroker's office, a fruit merchant, a blacksmith, a musician, a chair manufacturer and a glass engraver. They were all accompanied by their wives, and two small children, as well as a boy aged 18 and four young women, one of whom had been about to be married when she fled her home. Her fiancé was also a refugee somewhere in the south of England.

BELGIAN REFUGEES, MIDDLESBROUGH 1914

A very rare image of the Belgian refugees at the house in Woodlands Road, Middlesbrough, shortly after their arrival there in September 1914. (Courtesy of the Evening Gazette, Middlesbrough)

The party was met with a shake of hands by a number of prominent citizens, including the mayor, and Penry Williams with his wife. After being ushered into a quiet waiting room, the mayor addressed them, offering them a warm welcome and sympathising with their plight. He also spoke of having travelled around Belgium himself. As his words were translated to the Belgians by Rev. J Claus, secretary to the Bishop of Middlesbrough, tears of gratitude filled their eyes. Following a reply by one of the refugees who spoke in French, the Belgians were taken to the station yard where motor cars, cabs and small brakes stood waiting for them. The Belgian men, with a doffing of hats, acknowledged a rousing cheer from the waiting crowd.

They were taken to various destinations, where hot meals awaited them. One family went to Pinchinthorpe Hall as the guest of Penry Williams and his wife; another went to Normanby Hall as guests of Penry's brother, Illtyd Williams; whilst four people from Louvain went to a cottage in Swainby, belonging to Miss Elizabeth Wright of 111 Albert Road, Middlesbrough; the remainder went to William Meggeson's house in Woodlands Road.

Make Yourself at Home

After a good night's sleep they all gathered together again on Sunday morning to attend mass at St Mary's Cathedral, where the Archbishop of York, Dr Cosmo Lang, on a four day visit to Middlesbrough, preached the sermon. Later in the afternoon, the Archbishop, along with the mayor and a small party, visited the Belgians at the house in Woodlands Road where they were staying. There, he addressed them in their own language. Before the Archbishop left, one of the Belgians, Mr Charles Seys, came forward and read an address of thanks, but was so deeply touched he broke down before he reached the end. Tragically Mr Seys, who was an accountant from Malines, died suddenly from a heart attack a few days later leaving behind him in Middlesbrough a wife, two daughters and a grandchild aged only 6 months. He also left another daughter behind in Brussels who was a teacher, but had been prevented from leaving by the Germans. Mr Seys was buried in the cemetery of St Joseph's Church, North Ormesby. As a mark of respect, the mayor attended the funeral, where the coffin carried by his fellow refugees had a wreath in the Belgian national colours placed upon it.

Middlesbrough continued to take its Belgian refugees to its heart. So many people wanted to see them that visiting had to be restricted to 3–5 p.m. Donations of gifts and offers of help poured in to the Belgian Refugee Committee. On 18 October, meetings at the Grove Hill and Newport Allotment Holders Association Club decided unanimously to send weekly parcels of their vegetables to the Belgians living in the town.

Another meeting, on 19 October at the schoolroom in Westerdale, following an appeal by the Rev. C.W. James, Rector of the parish, decided that they would support the offer of Mrs Wood of Middlesbrough to allow some Belgians to live in 'The Bungalow', her summer residence in the village.

Tom McIntosh, the secretary of Middlesbrough Football Club announced that the directors had decided to donate £50 to the Belgian Relief Fund. Other firms and companies also contributed regularly to the fund. In many cases, the works switched their funding from local distress cases since work was more plentiful now. By the courtesy of the manager, J. Imeson, thirty refugees went to see a performance of Robert Courtneidge's musical comedy 'Oh, Oh, Delphine' at the Grand Opera House, starring Ruby Vyvyan as Delphine. The ladies received chocolates and the gentlemen refreshments and cigarettes. During the interval the national anthems of the Allies were sung, with the performers holding flags of both countries as the audience stood to sing. The *North-Eastern Daily Gazette* even printed a letter from the Consul-General for Belgium in London, in their own language, with news of home.

Despite the mass of donations for the refugees, more money was needed. At a meeting in the Town Hall, led by the mayor, with the Belgians present sitting in the central row of seats, ideas were discussed for fund raising. Middlesbrough had raised £1,000 for the Belgian Fund, but none of that could be used for local purposes. It was decided to hold a 'Flag Day' on Saturday, 17 October 1914. Many different people in the town became involved, led by the town's sportsmen including the secretary manager of Middlesbrough Football Club, Tom McIntosh. The aim was to sell 60,000 flag badges designed to look like small brooches. Tradesmen were asked to hang out the Belgian flag and five barrel organs, lent free by the Scappaticci family were paraded through the streets, raising over £20.

The Flag Day became a great triumph, with the whole town festooned with black, red and yellow bunting. Almost everyone seemed to have a flag badge. Newspaper boys sold them free of commission, whilst some large shops, including Wright & Co., Dickson & Benson and Newhouse & Sons, allowed special stalls in their stores to sell the flag badges. Flag sellers neglected no thoroughfare, and the football ground, Ayresome Park, where 25,000 people

Highlights of a flag day, held on 17 October 1914 to raise money for the Belgian refugees, were depicted in a cartoon in the North-Eastern Daily Gazette. *(Courtesy of the* Evening Gazette, Middlesbrough)

117

gathered to watch Middlesbrough's 1–1 draw against Newcastle United, was a scene of great activity, with thousands of flags being sold. When some of the specially invited Belgian refugees in the crowd appeared on the pitch before the game, there were rousing emotional scenes.

The glamorous French artiste and singer Liane D'Eve, who was appearing at the Empire for a week, agreed to sell Belgian flags on the streets of Middlesbrough on behalf of the Refugees Fund. In fact D'Eve was the most successful collector on the day, raising over £20. Over 80,000 flags were eventually sold, with the highest price paid for a single flag being £2 – a week's wages for many workers in industry. A total of £709 18s 11d (£709.94) was raised, and after deduction for the purchase of the flags, a profit of £591 7s 9d (£591.34) was declared – £500 of which was sent to the National Belgian Fund, and the remainder presented to the Middlesbrough Belgian Refugee Fund.

Support for the Belgian refugees continued throughout the war, under the auspices of the Fund for Housing Belgian Refugees Committee. In recognition of the help and assistance given to the refugees, the King of Belgium conferred the 'Medaille de la Reine Elizabeth' upon two of the leading figures in the campaign, Mrs W.J. Bruce and Mrs J. McCreton.

Wartime Entertainment and Sport

Like tourism, the world of entertainment faced problems in the immediate days following the start of war. The most popular entertainment in the town was football, and the new professional football season for Middlesbrough FC began as usual, on Tuesday 1 September, with a 3–1 defeat away at Sheffield Wednesday before a crowd of 12,000. Whilst there was some criticism in the press about continuing the season, a counter argument was that the Football Association and Football League governed the players and officials of Middlesbrough FC, meaning they had to obey their ruling or suffer heavy penalties.

There were strict instructions issued regarding contributions from practice matches being sent to the Prince of Wales National Relief Fund, and Middlesbrough accordingly sent £70 4s (£70.20). They also sent money to various other causes including £26 8s 3d (£26.42) to North Riding Infirmary and £20 to North Ormesby Hospital.

The war was never very far away, with many criticisms about football being allowed to continue. When Middlesbrough played their first home game on 5 September 1914, defeating West Bromwich Albion 2–0 before a crowd of 12,000 spectators, there were constant reminders of the war with a military parade at half-time and a recruitment meeting in the North Stand at the end of the game.

At a meeting held at the Pack Horse Hotel, Bolton, on 7 September, the Football League management committee confirmed in reply to the request to stop football that, after discussions with clubs, football would continue. One man who wanted football to continue was Chief Constable Henry Riches, who commented several times in court that there was less drunkenness in Middlesbrough when the Boro played at home. Men who had joined up were certainly happy that football was continuing. They wrote many letters back to the *Sports Gazette* (published on a Saturday evening by the *North-Eastern Daily Gazette*) talking of football games or conversations they had enjoyed with other fans – even in the trenches on the front line!

As the campaign to recruit men for Kitchener's Army continued throughout autumn 1914, the pressure on young men to enlist increased. Even the *Sports Gazette*'s leading columnist, who wrote under the pseudonym 'Old Bird' said, under a large headline 'Old Bird's Appeal To Young Men', that young men should be joining up, calling for the Football Association to ban young unmarried men from watching football games. One club, Aston Villa, had taken the lead by exhorting any players eligible to enlist to do so immediately. Elsewhere, eleven players in the Scottish team, Hearts of Midlothian, had enlisted. After the formation of a Footballers' Battalion in December 1914, Middlesbrough Football Club received a letter to ask if any players would join. The directors asked club captain, Andrew Jackson, to ask if any of the team wished to join. Jackson received a further letter on 6 April 1915 asking him to persuade teammates to join the undersubscribed Footballers' Battalion.

A meeting of the board of directors at Middlesbrough FC, on 10 December 1914, decided that 'in the event of any players who wanted to join the Teesside Battalion and the War Office sanctioning their playing to the end of the season, the directors are prepared to carry out the terms of the present signed contracts'. Players were told that the directors would be happy to discuss individual cases.

Four first team players joined up, along with the manager Tom McIntosh but, as they were still able to play, the club completed its fixtures, finishing with an away game at Blackburn Rovers on 24 April 1915. Three members of that team on the final day were later killed in the war.

With the season having been completed, the club awaited a decision regarding the next season. This came at a meeting on 19 July 1915, attended by club director, Harry French. Three days later, he reported back to his fellow directors at Middlesbrough that League football would not be played the following season. Although various regional leagues were formed, Middlesbrough didn't join them and apart from occasional 'exhibition' friendlies, no official games were played at Ayresome Park until 1919. In fact, the ground was used by the military for some time and was returned to the club just before games restarted.

Other popular sports fared less well. One of the big questions was whether or not Stockton Race Week would be held, and would local works shut down for the week as was their normal custom? The *North-Eastern Daily Gazette* did a survey of local businesses and found that most iron works were closing, whilst shipping companies were keeping open. Unions, such as the Boilermakers' Society, said they wouldn't stand in the way of any members who wished to work. In the event, the *North-Eastern Daily Gazette* officially announced on Monday 10 August that Stockton Races had been abandoned. Racing at Redcar was also cancelled. The traditional Stockton Race Week took place again on 27 August 1917 when record crowds, pleased to be back, flocked to the course.

The town's main entertainment venues struggled for a while, too. J.C Imeson, manager at the Grand Opera House spoke of the crisis in the theatrical world, where the problems with transport and men enlisting were throwing arrangements for the autumn programme into chaos, and many touring managers had simply abandoned their autumn tours. The Opera House had been due to reopen on 17 August, with Louis Meyer's company performing 'Who's the Lady?', but Meyer had pulled out only five days before it was due to begin. He had also planned to pull out of the next engagement, 'Mr Wu', a gripping drama which had just completed a nine month run at the Strand Theatre, London, and had been seen by King George V and Queen Mary on 16 February. To address this crisis, the Grand Opera House offered a special programme entitled 'War Scenes in Belgium' on 24 August. Although this was essentially censored material, it nevertheless drew heavily on the huge public sympathy for the plight of the Belgians – a clever marketing move by Imeson.

As the town's theatres began to adapt they had to come up with innovative ways to produce and present entertainment. Many shows had a war theme, or were directly involved with the war itself. These included recruitment meetings and appearances by celebrity figures from the world of entertainment or from politics. In mid-September a programme of patriotic Sunday evening concerts began. These were staged at a different theatrical venue each week, and followed a similar format by offering a lecture on the war (or some other similar event) and then the singing of patriotic songs. Doors opened at 8 p.m. and all proceeds went to the Prince of Wales National Relief Fund. Gradually more (censored) film material from the Front became available. The War Office film 'The Battle of the Somme' was proudly shown to packed houses at the Hippodrome from Monday 16 October to Wednesday 18 October 1916. The theatre described it as showing in a 'vivid manner, the heroic work of our gallant lads … [who] even when the wounded returned still had the strength to smile and have a cigarette'. Another film from the Front was 'Britain Prepared – a Kinematograph Review of … the Military' which brought capacity crowds to the Grand Opera House in the week before Christmas 1916, as did 'With the French on the Somme' at the Hippodrome.

BACK TO BLIGHTY

Very soon after the first action at the Front, at Mons, transportation of the wounded soldiers back to England began in earnest. For authorities in England one of the most pressing duties was preparing for the arrival of wounded soldiers from Belgium and France. With no co-ordinated national health service, other agencies had to take on this role.

In the early days of the war there was a great deal of willingness to help, and many local hospitals offered the use of their facilities. The British Red Cross Society who, having joined forces with the Order of St John Ambulance to form the Joint War Committee, were empowered to raise Voluntary Aid Detachments, under the War Office Voluntary Aid Scheme. Members (individuals were called 'detachments' or VAD's) were trained in first aid, nursing, cookery, hygiene and sanitation. Men were also trained in first aid and stretcher bearing. The Middlesbrough St John's Ambulance group eventually helped train over 2,500 people in first aid and nursing during the war. As increasing numbers of trained nursing staff went out to field hospitals abroad, VAD's became their essential replacements.

Nº 4 Wounded British Soldiers & Nursing Staff.
Manor House Hospital Stokesley

(Author's collection)

5

'Tea or Munitions, We're here to Help!'

'We're Here to Help'

There is a common misconception that, when war was declared in 1914, everybody in Britain adopted a tough 'John Bull' resolve and, having decided to fight, just 'got on with it' until victory was achieved in 1918. This is, of course, a total myth and, whilst there is certainly copious evidence of resolve, grit and determination shown throughout the four years of conflict, there are also suggestions that there was a great deal of misery and distress too.

Leaving aside for one moment the physical injuries, there were a lot of people who, without the help provided by the multitude of organisations, committees and other support agencies, would have simply found the struggles of wartime life almost impossible to endure.

In Middlesbrough, almost from the start of the war, numerous families were suddenly left without financial support. Soldiers who joined up received £5, whilst their wives got 1*s* (5p) per day and 7*d* (2.5p) for each child during his absence. However, due to the sheer number of men joining up and an inefficient system, it was several weeks before dependents received any allowances. Many casual labourers, particularly those who worked on the river, were made unemployed in the early days of the war when local industry and shipping ground to a halt.

Clearly this was a problem. Whether it was men joining up or suddenly facing unemployment, there was the question of how best to ease the destitution suddenly faced by many families. On 6 August Sir Hugh Bell, Lord Lieutenant of the North Riding, wrote to the mayor about the formation of local committees to help deal with these cases. He also suggested waiting until national guidance was given on these matters. Local industry acted quickly to ease the problems. Bolckow, Vaughan and Co. Ltd announced, on 11 August, that they would pay any employees who were married or had dependents a weekly allowance of half of their earnings up to £1 per week, and those who were unmarried and without dependents, an allowance equal to one third of their wage, not exceeding 13*s* 4*d* (67p) per week. Workmen at Harkess and Sons shipyard in Middlesbrough took a unanimous decision to contribute 3*d* (1.5p) in the pound each week, towards the support of local wives and families of men who had gone to war.

It was reported on 13 August that there was a considerable amount of distress in Middlesbrough, with many wives of reservists being left destitute, and the wives of riverside workers now unemployed were also suffering. Providing some relief was now urgent, so the mayor enlisted the aid of the 'Guild of Help', who had previously assisted during the Coal Strike of 1912. At the offices of the Guild of Help, a staff of twelve dealt with over 300 cases between 10 a.m. and 12 noon. There were so many that they had to move to a larger office in the Town Hall Crypt the following day. There were long queues, which were not helped by unemployed men mistakenly trying to get their benefits when they should have gone to the Labour Exchange first. By 14 August over 700 names were registered, and by Monday, 17 August, the total had reached 800, nearly all of those being the wives of men on active service or unemployed riverside men.

Under instructions from the Local Government Board, the mayor formed a local 'General Distress Committee'. There were some protests voiced over the way that the committee had been set up. In a fit of political pique, the Middlesbrough Board of Guardians heavily criticised the mayor for not consulting them regarding which of their members sat on the relief committee – even though he had only been acting at the request of the Local Government Board. Other complaints came from the Independent Labour Party who, having passed a resolution on 11 August condemning the war as being 'the fault of Cabinet Ministers in the past', now said angrily that they too were not represented on the committee. The *North-Eastern Daily Gazette* suggested with some irritation that 'this was not a time to bother about nice distinctions but [a time] to get to work'.

Alice Schofield Coates voiced criticisms from the Women's Suffrage National Aid Corps (Women's Freedom League) that there was no attempt to represent women, other than those connected with charitable organisations. She argued that it was:

> … not from the well-to-do members of the charity organisations that you will find the best means of helping women who have the duty of keeping a home together while the men are away or out of employment.

Many letters confirmed strong support for the mayor, with most people accepting that he was 'following orders'. The 'well-to-do members' making items had a lot of support too – public opinion concluding that at least they were doing something, rather than just complaining.

As the immediate impact of the war lessened, river traffic returned to some sort of normality, industry adjusted to the new trading conditions and the unemployed men gradually returned to work. By 1 September there was a decrease in the number of cases of distress, with the number of new applications now down to thirty per day. The Guild of Help had 1,370 names on the register, but the majority of those did not need relief since service pay was now coming through. The cases dealing with dock and riverside workers had almost all been closed as work on the river was plentiful once more.

There was other work to do though, as many dependents of those who had enlisted or been called up were still waiting for any form of allowance to come through. By 25 September over 2,000 cases had been investigated and relieved – many of whom had been wives and dependents of men on active war service. Regrettably, human nature being what it is, there were some cases of people trying to claim war relief under false pretences. One woman told the Guild of Help that her son was in the Territorials and claimed relief – this was true, but it was proved he had never contributed to his keep when he was at home anyway! Citing the case as an example to the public, Alderman W.J. Bruce imprisoned her for two days.

A controversial letter from Robert Bell, an accountant based at Cleveland Chambers, Borough Road West, appeared in the *North-Eastern Daily Gazette* on 2 October, stating that they had four cases of distress with sons or fathers either away at the Front, or in training for one month to six weeks, yet dependents were still without money from the War Office. Bell called for something to be done – forcing the mayor to reply on 5 October, also through a letter to the *Gazette*, that in all these four cases things *were* being done. In giving the detailed facts about each case, he reminded Bell that in many cases the individuals them- selves were to blame for not giving the correct information according to the instructions. The town clerk and the mayor had written to commanding officers across the country, to expedite without delay the necessary papers to expedite payments. In the meantime, the mayor had issued the previous Saturday a payment of 10*s* (50p) to 180 women in order to tide them over.

Bell replied through the paper to say that he appreciated the job being done, and it was not his aim to harass the mayor, but it was very difficult for a woman with seven children to live on 10*s* (50p) per week. He said it was their job to get these on to the War Office list which was, happily, due to begin the next week. The mayor acted very quickly to successfully clarify this situation, with the Middlebrough Recruiting Committee refusing to support the government's recruitment campaigns until the situation was remedied.

Committees for Everything

Financial donations were not the only aid being provided. Those who volunteered received a lot of support from the town. The Middlesbrough YMCA opened their rooms at the corner of Albert Terrace and Linthorpe Road to all service men. The rooms had facilities for reading, games, letter writing and smoking. Military personnel were also allowed free use of Middlesbrough Corporation Baths.

The exhibition of the famous Bairnsfather sketches and Raemaeker's cartoons in January 1917, was one of many events held to raise money during the war. (Courtesy of the Evening Gazette, Middlesbrough)

Assistance took several other forms, typified by the Middlesbrough Hospital and Clothing Committee. On 12 August, Mayoress Mary Bruce chaired a very large gathering of ladies at the Town Hall, Middlesbrough, where a committee was appointed to oversee the making of underclothing for wounded soldiers, and clothing for those families of reservists who had been left inadequately provided for. Mary Bruce was elected president, Elsie Harkess was made secretary, and a room was found for use in the Town Hall. A subscription list was opened, but the ladies who joined would not only be asked to donate materials they would be required to do the actual work. Anyone wanting to assist could contact the Town Hall. Garments and bed clothing could be dropped at the Town Hall's Albert Road entrance. A number of ladies quickly volunteered to come and sew. Donations included mattresses, pillows, socks, and towels.

Events to support the funds went on throughout the war. One notable event was the exhibiting of a captured German gun, which was brought to the town on

Public Notices.

MAYOR'S RELIEF FUND.

TOWN HALL, MIDDLESBRO'.
MONDAY, JANUARY 8, AND DAILY
UNTIL SATURDAY, 13th.

EXHIBITION

OF

RAEMAEKERS CARTOONS,

BAIRNSFATHER SKETCHES,

CLEVELAND SKETCHING CLUB
EXHIBITION.

CLEVELAND CAMERA CLUB
EXHIBITION.

WAR RELICS,

MUSICAL ENTERTAINMENTS.

TO BE OPENED ON MONDAY, AT 2.30, BY

LADY PEASE.

ADMISSION to Opening, 2s 6d; 6 to 9, 1s. Tuesday, Wednesday, Thursday, Friday, 2.30, to 6
1s; 6 to 9, 6d. Saturday, All Day, 6d. Season
Tickets, 5s.

22 January 1916. The gun, a 13-pounder with a 3in bore, had inscribed on the shield, '15th Division, Loos, 25th', and 'Nr. 13, Fr. Kp gef 1897, Fr. Kp. Obg 1908 Sg J.' inscribed on the breech. Originally it was to be exhibited in the centre of town to encourage recruitment, but it was considered that 'more than a passing interest' might be taken in the gun, so it went on display in the Drill Hall in Grange Road where it helped raise money for the Central Relief Fund.

Another significant event was the exhibition of cartoons by the world famous Dutch artist, Louis Raemaekers, in Middlesbrough Town Hall from Monday, 8 January, to Saturday, 13 January 1917, to raise money for the mayor's Central Relief Fund. There was also a display of the famous original 'Bairnsfather Sketches', loaned by the *Bystander* magazine. The event was opened by Sir Alfred Pease and, despite stormy weather that week, attracted good crowds. Other events included a 'Patriotic Shopping Week', when shopkeepers in the town contributed a sum equal to the amount that was spent in their shops, with a 'Window Dressing' competition held at the same time.

The Relief Fund was used to help in many ways; one of the more unusual was contributing to the cost of a hospital bed in the Anglo–Russian Hospital in Petrograd. As well as a photograph of the 'Middlesbrough Bed' occupied by a patient, Czarina Alexandra sent a letter of thanks to Mayor J. Calvert. The photograph was framed and displayed in the Town Hall.

In January 1918, one event that really caught the interest of the town was 'Tank Week'. Mayor J. Calvert was informed by the brigadier general in command of the Teesside area that the tank, *Nelson* (No 130), previously displayed in Trafalgar Square, London, would make a week-long visit to Middlesbrough from 14 January to help raise money for the newly introduced Government War Loans. Many people couldn't get into the War Bond meeting held at the Hippodrome Theatre the night before the event began, but 3,500 people, including all of the town's prominent figures, listened to speeches from the mayor and other dignitaries. Lt E. Spence reminded the crowd how far the town had come since the first outdoor recruitment meeting at

MIDDLESBROUGH SOLDIERS ARE DOING *THEIR* DUTY!

GRAND ORCHESTRAL CONCERT,
CINEMATOGRAPH ENTERTAINMENT,
AND

"TANK" WAR BOND MEETING,

SUNDAY, JANUARY 13TH, 1918,
AT THE

HIPPODROME, MIDDLESBRO'

(By the kindness and courtesy of COUNCILLOR THOMAS THOMSON,
The Chair will be taken at 6 p.m. prompt by the
MAYOR OF MIDDLESBROUGH,
Supported by the War Savings Committee
and the Officers of the TANK "NELSON."

SPEAKERS:
LIEUT. E. SPENCE, W. H. THOMAS, ESQ., AND
CORPL. BRANDON a Member of the Tank Crew),
who will give a Vivid Account of his Experience
with the Tanks in Action.

ALL SEATS FREE.   DOORS OPEN, 7.30 P.M.

PTE. TOM DRESSER, V.C.

NOW IS THE CHANCE FOR MIDDLESBROUGH PEOPLE TO DO THEIRS!

A postcard published to promote the Middlesbrough Tank Week, in January 1918. (Author's collection)

Infirmary Corner in 1914. As always, Spence roused the crowd with his words, ending by asking all those who were willing to pledge themselves to stand up. They did, and then remained standing as the last speaker was Corporal Brandon, a member of the tank crew who had driven it at the Front. He stood up to give a rousing speech and his stirring words were given rapturous applause.

The tank was given a spectacular welcome when it arrived from Hull and was placed near the Bolckow Statue on Marton Road. On a cold Monday morning in January, a long procession was led by mounted police. Civic dignitaries including MP Penry Williams, Mayor J. Calvert and the Lord Lieutenant Sir Hugh Bell, were joined by bands from several regiments. A huge crowd watched the procession leave Russell Street and proceed via Albert Road, Borough Road, Linthorpe Road and Zetland Road into Marton Road to the site of the tank.

At 11 a.m. Sir Hugh Bell mounted the dais, unfurled the Union Jack and gave a salute. Then the mayor ascended to the top of the tank and spoke briefly to the huge crowd. The crowd roared with laughter when he said that the tank had come a long way and 'had a very capacious mouth and [he] hoped the people of Middlesbrough would feed it liberally this week … with 5 per cent or 4 per cent War Bonds or the humble 15s 6d (77p) War Certificate'. Parodying the words associated with the name of Nelson, Mayor J. Calvert received loud applause when he said he hoped 'everyone in Middlesbrough would do their duty'. Sir Hugh Bell took the first certificate, and then the mayor announced that a number of donations, to the sum of £800,000, had already been received. Then it was over to the people of the town.

The 'Tank Bank', as it became known, was open from 10 a.m. to 8 p.m. and it was illuminated at night. Special events took place each day as the tank crew told tales of life at the Front. By Tuesday evening the total had reached £1,094,232 and by the end of the week had reached £1,957,232, a record for a town of Middlesbrough's size. On the final evening the mayor once again climbed up to the top of the tank, a 'unique platform' as the *North-Eastern Daily Gazette* called it, to thank all of the town and the tank crew for a wonderful week. The evening finished with the band of the Welsh Regiment playing the national anthem, loudly accompanied by the large crowd. When the ceremony closed many stayed behind to watch the tank move into Wilson Street on the way to the station. The *North-Eastern Daily Gazette* reported that:

> The engines of the tank began to throb and Nelson … snorted once more and heaved itself on the barricade … there was great joy as … Nelson performed its cater-pillar movements along Wilson Street, Albert Road and Bridge Street to the Goods Station [where] it got a rousing cheer and a happy send off to Sunderland.

There were so many agencies that gave aid in many different ways during the war, that it is impossible within this publication than to give more than brief details. Table 3 attempts to address this task with information on the main organisations operating during this period:

Table 3: Aid agencies, Middlesbrough area 1914–19

Organisation	Date Operated From	Person i/c (President or Organiser)	Comments
Guild of Help	1914	Mayor W.J. Bruce	Broad remit dealing with cases of distress in the town.
Soldiers & Sailors Association	1914	Mrs J.W. Pennyman & Mrs Hedley	Along with Guild of Help, gave financial support to dependents of the military – crucial in 1914 when many wives waited so long for separation allowances that they had to survive on grants.
British Red Cross 29th Yorks VAD, Middlesbrough	1914	Dr G.F. Longbotham	Originally formed 11 April 1914 – conveyed 4,000 wounded soldiers who came to town. Worked with Hemlington Hospital.
British Red Cross Working Parties Nos 4,033 & 5,758	1914	Mrs C.J. Sambridge	Raised funds & made over 2,500 garments to send to British Red Cross Headquarters.
Prince of Wales National Relief Fund	1914	Mayor W.J. Bruce & Mayor J. Calvert	£17,587 subscribed by Middlesbrough. £1,636 given to 4,400 local cases. £15,951 sent to fund in London.
Vegetables for the Fleet	1914	Lady Bell of Rounton Grange	Sent vegetables to River Tees naval base.
Middlesbrough Hospital & Clothing Fund	1914	Mayoress Bruce	Made items for those in hospital and took in contributions from public. Merged with Voluntary Workers Association 1915.
Disabled, Discharged & Fallen Military & Dependents Fund	1914	Alderman R. Archibald JP	£1,250 subscribed by Alderman & Mrs Roddam Dent. Assistance given from interest.
Entertainment Committee – Hemlington Hospital	1914	Alfred Smith	Organised concerts/entertainment for wounded soldiers. Funded (£570) by Middlesbrough Central War Relief Fund.
Middlesbrough War Heroes Fund	1914	Councillor E. Turner	To reward local war heroes.
Middlesbrough Voluntary Workers Association	1914	Mayoress Calvert	Co-ordinated the making of 11,000 clothing items by schools, for men on service.
Cleveland War Hospital Work Guild	1914	Lady Dorman of Grey Towers	Guild of fifty members made & distributed 57,696 articles to naval & military hospitals, home & abroad.

Fund for Housing Belgian Refugees	1914	Mayor W.J. Bruce	Organised fundraising/housing for Belgian refugees in Middlesbrough.
Mayor's Private Local Relief Fund	1914	Mayor J. Calvert	Financial assistance to those who couldn't claim through other ways.
Middlesbrough Local War Savings Committee	1914	Mayor J. Calvert	Raised £13,395,365 for War Loans through subscriptions & events including: Victory Loan – £1,979,423 Tank Week – £1,957,797 Feed the Guns week – £1,624,602 Business Men's week – £533,142 Chamber of Trade week – £123,475.
Winter Garden War Knitting	1914	Mayoress Calvert & Lady Bell	Sent knitted articles of clothing to prisoners of war. Also raised funds for wounded military personnel.
Mayor's Central War Relief Fund	1915	Mayor J. Calvert	Raising money from business firms, tradesmen, industry & private citizens to make donations to War Relief Fund and other war charities. A total of £12,836 was raised. Major donations included: British Red Cross – £1,393 Belgian Relief Fund – £800 Hemlington Hospital Soldiers – £570 YMCA Huts – £650 RSPCA – Wounded Animals – £250.
Local Prisoners of War Fund	1915	Mrs A. Mattison	Sent food, cigarettes & clothes to sixty-three prisoners of war from local area.
Middlesbrough Maternity & Infant Welfare Committee	1915	Mayor J. Calvert	Provided facilities to help and support those in need, especially during the food shortages.
Middlesbrough Church Of England & Free Church Canteens	1916	Mrs Hedley	Two popular canteen facilities for soldiers and sailors. On Armistice Night almost 900 men were served. Established by subscriptions.
Naval & Military War Pensions Committee	1916	Mayor J. Calvert	Assisted with over 14,000 cases.
Queen Mary's Needlework Guild, Middlesbrough	1916	Mrs Hedley	Made 62,754 articles for surgical requisites and hospital necessities. These were dispatched to the Front. Existed entirely on private donations.
Middlesbrough Schools	1917	School Head Teachers	Sandbags made by pupils in schools sent for use at the Front

Middlesbrough Local Food Committee	1917	Mayor J. Calvert	Systematic control of food supply. Issued ration cards & established: Sugar rationing. Local Food Distribution Scheme. National Rationing Scheme – including meat, milk, cheese, jam, butter, sugar for jam preserving, tea, flour & bread, potatoes, bacon, ham, lard, fish. Communal kitchens – in the old Police Station & St Paul's Mission Hall, Cannon Street.
Middlesbrough Local Advisory Committee	1918	Mayor J. Calvert	Helped in absorption of demobilised men back into employment.
Middlesbrough Local Fuel & Lighting Committee	1918	Alderman Amos Hinton	Ensuring adequate fuel supplies available to all.

Help was also given to other social problems that arose during wartime. Middlesbrough had always had a large number of public houses, and despite the restrictions of licensing hours under DORA there were a rising number of incidents of drunkenness, especially convictions of women, throughout the war. Various organisations, including the Temperance Movement tried to tackle this problem.

Another organisation trying to help men was the Winter Garden, in Dundas Street. It was the idea of Lady Florence Bell, and first opened on 24 October 1907 to offer the men of Middlesbrough, 'everything possible to make their hours of leisure comfortable'. The Winter Garden, with its cheap entrance fee of 1*d* (one penny) and tea and biscuits for the same price, offered a range of pastimes and entertainments between October and May, including Sunday evening music concerts that were considered to be more 'uplifting and cultured'. With the doors opening at 9 a.m. and not closing till 10 p.m. it attracted large numbers of patrons. The annual report for the Winter Garden published in September 1914 showed that 57,497 people had used the facility during the 1913–14 season, 236 per day on average.

The Winter Garden depended on subscriptions to make it financially viable, but with many other causes asking for money subscriptions fell in the first year of the war, and there was a deficit for the first time in August 1915 of £33 2s 3d (£33.11). The fortitude of Lady Bell turned this into a profit of £114 in 1916, and £106 in 1917 when the Winter Garden celebrated its tenth anniversary. With free entrance for men in uniform, the venue was very popular with the military – 3,218 soldiers visited in 1917. From 1915, a group of Middlesbrough ladies also met at the Winter Garden to knit garments to send off to soldiers and the Red Cross. Following the receipt of a postcard from seven British prisoners of war in Germany they organised three cases of materials to be sent to them. Three years later, one of the group arrived at the Winter Garden to thank them for the things they had sent.

The Tipperary Rooms, which were opened by Lady Zetland in a house in St Paul's Terrace, Newport Road, on 12 March 1915, offered support to the wives, mothers and sisters of service men. It was hoped that this would deter women from the temptations of 'the public house and private drinking'. Like the Winter Garden for men, it provided a retreat from the stress of the war, and facilities included subsidised cheap refreshments, a library, savings bank and a nursery for children. There were regular concerts each week and over the summer there were various events for the women and their children, including picnics at Grey Towers in Nunthorpe, the home of Sir Arthur Dorman. When food became short the committee managed to supplement the supply of milk. Talks on subjects such as hygiene, nursing and 'thrift' were also given to the women.

There was growing concern during the war about women beyond these organisations. In 1917 a female patrol force was formed to 'manage' and advise any girls who were on the streets regarding 'inappropriate behaviour', with female Special Constables patrolling the streets in areas where there were canteens, or soldiers billeted. In recognition of the problem, on 23 April 1918, Middlesbrough appointed Miss H. Owens, a female probation officer, to tackle the growing problems of female offenders.

Juveniles and Schools in Wartime

Despite a late return after the summer holiday of 1914, schools tried to continue as normally as they could whilst adapting to changes caused by the war. From October 1915, afternoon lessons began earlier due to the lighting restrictions – this allowed the caretakers more daylight time for cleaning duties. Class sizes increased due to difficulties replacing male teachers who had enlisted. Teachers at Grange Road Infants went 'en masse' to see the head to complain when class numbers reached sixty-eight children.

It is interesting to note in the Middlesbrough High School for Girls log book, that two Belgian children started there on 27 October 1914.

Three stern-looking schoolboys in front of a load of sacking used by schoolchildren to make up sandbags – their part in the war effort. (Courtesy of the Dorman Museum)

On 7 April 1916 the attendance at Ayresome School Senior is recorded as being 'very low due to the Zeppelin raid'. Just over a month later the whole school assembled 'in the hall to witness the school clock being put forward an hour' marking the start of British Summer Time for the very first time. On 14 December 1916 Ayresome School Senior was taken over by the military, and all pupils moved to the Park Wesley

Sunday School, which meant one outside toilet for 425 children. It returned to its own premises in the summer of 1917.

The increase in juvenile crime throughout the war period caused some concern. On 27 June 1916 the *North-Eastern Daily Gazette* highlighted the reasons for the increase and called for a coordinated approach to the problem. Chief Constable Henry Riches, in his annual report in March 1917 stated that there had been a 21 per cent rise in indictable offences – mainly committed by juveniles. It was felt that, with many fathers and other strong male figures away at the Front and many mothers working to help the war effort, some children were subject to less direct parenting and discipline at home.

There was an attempt to involve children in the war effort. On 23 February 1917, the head of Ayresome Senior School, Mr J. Adams, records in the school logbook that 'the whole afternoon was spent making sacks for the military'. An entry for 11 May 1917, records that 'pupils have completed: 2,738 sandbags, 2,570 grenade bags, 200 pairs of socks and mittens. A number of boys have on several occasions, attended Kirby School allotment to help plant potatoes.' In one school, the girls made over 2,000 garments for troops and sent £10 to the British Red Cross.

Middlesbrough High School Scouts helped in many different ways, ranging from assisting guards at Redcar and Saltburn during the school holidays to giving out leaflets for the War Savings Committee, and working as orderlies. When heavy snow fell in March 1917, it was boys from the High School who cleared the streets in Middlesbrough. Schools helped in fundraising activities, including 'Tank Week' in January 1918.

Teachers also suffered the stress of war. In February 1918 schools began 'air-raid drills'. In the same week, the school logbook notes that one teacher, Mrs Longden, was given time off to spend some hours with her husband, briefly home on leave from France.

One common entry in all the school log books is the one for 11 November 1918, when the pupils were called into assembly just before lunch and dismissed for the rest of the day in honour of the Armistice being signed.

Prince of Wales Relief Fund

Donation forms for giving to the Prince of Wales National Relief Fund were published in the North-Eastern Daily Gazette *in 1914. (Courtesy of the* Evening Gazette, *Middlesbrough)*

As well as local fund raising, people in Middlesbrough and the surrounding area gave full support to the Prince of Wales National Relief Fund. The *North-Eastern Daily Gazette* printed lists of donors and the amount donated. The mayor headed the first list published on 18 August 1914, with other donations ranging from large amounts given by local businesses, to small individual collections, often from children, of only a few pence. A second list, then a third list, soon followed on 20 August 1914.

The National Relief Fund reached £1,000 on 22 August and over £2,000 by the end of August 1914. The *North-Eastern Daily Gazette* placed collection boxes around the town in shops, hotels, cafés etc. for people to drop their change into. Bolckow, Vaughan and Co. Ltd donated £1,000 to the fund and several other local firms encouraged employees to contribute money from their wages each week, including Lipton Ltd, staff at the Middlesbrough Goods Railway Station and Middlesbrough, Stockton and Thornaby Tramways Company.

Donations continued to pour in – seemingly from every person or organisation in the area. Collections taken at churches throughout the town were sent. The players and staff at Middlesbrough Football Club decided to contribute £3 per week, as well as donating the proceeds (entrance was 2*d*, 3*d*, or 4*d*) of their first practice game on 22 August. Club chairman, Phil Bach, made a private donation of 3 guineas (£3.15), whilst Arthur Bone, a hairdresser in Newport Road, gave one quarter of his takings for the month of September. The domestic staff at Southend, Grove Hill, one of the town's larger properties gave £1 12*s* (£1.60), whilst Ida Lithgow (aged 7) and Kathleen Field (aged 9) collected 3*s* (15p), the proceeds of a children's concert held on Redcar Sands at the hut of Mrs Lithgow. The list

A MIDDLESBROUGH APPEAL.

Are we "doing our bit" for the lads at the front,
And the bairns they have left at home?
Are we "doing our bit" for the sailormen,
Now keeping their watch o'er the foam?
We're waving the flag, we're shouting hooray!
We're marching the streets with the devil to pay,
But our soldiers and sailors may very well say,
Are we "doing our bit" at home?
It's not much they ask for the sacrifice made,
They're guarding our homes and protecting our trade;
It's the cheapest insurance that we ever paid,
By doing our "bit at home."

ALF. MATTISON.

The men at the works are nobly "doing their bit" for the dependents of the men who are fighting our battles by giving a sum weekly to the Fund. The Mayor (Alderman W. J. Bruce) feels that outside of the offices and works there are thousands of people of all ages and of varying circumstances who would happily give, according to their means, a weekly sum if a scheme was put on foot whereby their weekly subscriptions could be called for at their homes or places of business, and to further this object the Mayor appeals for assistance by helping to obtain a list of would-be subscribers. He suggests that persons desiring to give a weekly sum from a penny upwards should write their name and address, with the weekly amount to be given, on the form below and drop it into the collecting sheets or boxes which will be much in evidence in the Park on Saturday and Sunday.

With a view to furthering this object all those who are desirous of assisting are invited to attend a meeting to be held in the Town Hall on Thursday next, the 17th inst., at 7.30 p.m.

THE PRINCE OF WALES' NATIONAL RELIEF FFUND.

I am willing to assist the efforts being made in Middlesbrough to raise funds in aid of the above, and will subscribe

.... (state amount of contribution here) per week/month towards the same.

Name ....

Address ....

....

Day and time for collector to call for

donation ....day at ....

To the Town Clerk, Middlesbrough.

printed on 25 September features a donation of 12s 4d (62p) from Mr Wilson's dog, as well as a sum of £4 3s 10d (£4.19) collected by Mrs Armstrong's dog 'Vesta'. By way of contrast, the shipbuilders Raylton, Dixon & Co. Ltd donated £200.

Three days later, a huge procession of bands that had assembled in Borough Road marched to Albert Park in support of the Prince of Wales National Relief Fund, raising a total of £23 5s 7p (£23.27).

On 19 September 1914, the third week of the new term, the headmaster of Middlesbrough High School handed over the first weekly collection from his pupils, totalling 18s 5d (92.5p). Kirby School followed suit, and a collection from staff and pupils came to £2 3s 2d (£2.17).

Further afield, on 9 September 1914 a well-attended, enthusiastic meeting in the village schoolroom in Stainton decided to go around to every house to collect money for the fund. A meeting of the men employed on the Crathorne estate in North Yorkshire unanimously agreed to give a voluntary contribution to the fund, whilst residents in Commondale met in the council schoolroom and decided to give 3d (1.5p) per fortnight.

Colonel W.H.A. Wharton opened his home, Skelton Castle, on a Sunday afternoon with the aim of raising relief money. A large crowd attended, and they assembled in front of the castle and sang 'Abide with Me', followed by the national anthem, and cheered when the North Skelton Band played the 'Marseillaise'. Colonel Wharton addressed the crowd, pointing out the gravity of the situation and the need for young men to enlist.

Fundraising for the Prince of Wales National Relief Fund continued throughout the war with the final total raised by Middlesbrough being £17,587.

On 25 July 1917, a special matinee at the Grand Opera House celebrated Britain's Navy Week, all proceeds going to naval charities. All the artists gave their services for free and the mayoress sold the original of the programme cover by auction, with the mayor buying it for £20. (Courtesy of the Dorman Museum)

GRAND OPERA HOUSE
MIDDLESBOROUGH
KINDLY LENT BY
J.CHARLES IMESON ESQ.

NAVY WEEK

MATINEE
WEDNESDAY JULY 25TH
1917

After Lloyd George
spoke of the war being
fought in workshops,
skilled workers not
already involved in
government work could
register on an evening
at Middlesbrough
Town Hall.
This advert is from
the North-Eastern
Daily Gazette,
29 June 1915,
the first week of the
registration process.
(Courtesy of the
Evening Gazette,
Middlesbrough)

An Engineer's War, Munitions Required

David Lloyd George, speaking in Bangor on 28 February 1915, said 'the war would be fought in the workshops … under war conditions'.

Middlesbrough, with its rich heritage as a major centre of industry, particularly iron and steel, was well placed to take a crucial role in winning the war.

After the assertions of the British commander-in-chief, Sir John French, that the failure of the British offensive at Neuve Chappelle was due to a lack of shells, it was clear that British munitions production was not operating anywhere near full efficiency. With the 'Shell Crisis' still in mind, Lloyd George, minister for munitions in the new coalition government, reaffirmed in June that 'the engineers, employers and workmen of Britain can win this war. Without them victory is impossible.'

A campaign, including full page newspaper advertisements, began to improve the output of munitions. From 24 June 1915 any skilled workers not already involved in government work could register between 6 p.m. and 9 p.m., at Middlesbrough Town Hall, to volunteer for either munitions work or ship-building for the Admiralty. Once registered they were given a certificate for their employer informing them that the individual had enrolled as a war munitions volunteer, and they could be called upon to fill a post. In the first five days, seventy-nine men registered – a reasonable total considering many men in the town had either enlisted or were already engaged in government work.

Thos D. Ridley & Sons were contractors based in Middlesbrough who undertook general construction work including wharves, railways, docks etc., along with making and repairing small locomotives, boilers, cranes and other contractors' machinery in their engineering works. An employee, James Tait, suggested early in the war that the firm were capable of undertaking work in connection with the ministry of munitions. The firm then began to make 18-Pdr shrapnel shells for Messrs Vickers Ltd, of Sheffield. This led ultimately to the firm's repair shop in Louisa Street, North Ormesby, being turned into a munitions factory, and hydraulic presses installed for the making of forgings. Tait was later made a Member of the British Empire (MBE) for his work.

On 29 June 1915 there was a meeting of the Teesside Iron and Steel Makers & Engineers at the office of the Cleveland Ironmasters Association led by Colonel Hawdon, to discuss ways to increase the output of munitions. At the request of the chairman, T.D. Ridley explained how they were making shells with ordinary lathes, and said that if resources of all firms were utilised, output could be increased considerably. A local Teesside Munitions Committee was formed, with Thomas W. Ridley as chairman, for the purpose of

Mayor J. Calvert came to office in November 1915 and proceeded to lead the town through the rest of the war, unusually being in office for four years. (Courtesy of the Dorman Museum)

*'Filling Shop –
No 2 Shift'. Taken
at the works of
Thos D. Ridley
&Sons. Workers
featured are nearly
all women – making
munitions was a vital
part of the war effort.
(Courtesy of the
Dorman Museum)*

co-ordinating munitions work across the area and co-operating with the North-East Coast Armaments Committee to increase output of munitions.

Local employers with lathes were invited to inspect the process of manufacture of shells at Richardson-Westgarth's in respect of high explosives and at T.D. Ridley & Sons in respect of shrapnel. Ridley's increased their machine tools and erected a shed for the loading of the various shells made in the local area (most firms only did the machining, so Ridley's did the loading for all the others). This began a considerably busy period for local industry, led by the excellent pioneering work at T.D. Ridley & Sons.

'We Couldn't Have Done it Without You, Girls'

Throughout the war a large number of women came forward to offer their services – these included trained nurses, as well as ladies who just volunteered their labour. By August 1915 there were women porters at Middlesbrough Station, women delivering letters and milk – a situation that the *North-Eastern Daily Gazette* agreed was a 'change that has proved entirely satisfactory'.

These women are working on the construction of the Furness Shipyard at Haverton Hill. (Courtesy of Teesside Archives)

When the Military Service Act brought in conscription on 27 January 1916, the role of women became even more crucial, particularly in the workplace. Although the role of women workers in munitions is generally known, they also carried out roles in many other workplaces in the Middlesbrough area. Construction of the new Furness Shipyard at Haverton Hill employed a number of women workers undertaking heavy manual work.

Women were employed on a number of farms in the area too. The mayor informed a council meeting on 11 April 1916 that, after a recent meeting, over 100 women had volunteered to work on the land.

They worked in banks, offices, shops and factories. There were occasional problems, and when the work of women tram drivers on the route from Linthorpe to the Transporter Bridge was criticised, management replied that, despite overcrowded (tram) cars and worn brake gear, 'the young lady drivers were doing their best'.

Women War Workers: Middlesbrough 1914–19		
Munition workers working elsewhere (e.g. Gretna Green, Hereford, Leeds, Birmingham)	798	19.83%
Local munition workers	2,548	63.24%
Land workers	321	7.96%
Queen Mary's Army Auxiliary Corp (QMAAC)	289	7.17%
Navy & Army Canteen Board (NACB)	78	1.8%
Total	4,029	

More women working on the construction of the shipyard. Work started on the 85-acre site in 1917.
(Courtesy of Teesside Archives)

Further evidence of the remarkable contribution of women to industry. Two women in 1917 at the Roseberry Ironstone Mine, located on the southern flank of Roseberry Topping. The mine was worked 1880–83, then reworked 1907–24. (Courtesy of the Dorman Museum)

Football is a Women's Game, isn't it?

One of the unique aspects of the war prompted by the employ-ment of women was the rise of 'Munitionettes' football. The women employed at the factories had enough energy to kick a ball around during their breaks and, by 1917, a number of teams had been formed on Teesside and Tyneside. The traditional rivalry present in men's football soon transferred itself to the women's game, particularly amongst the various works teams in Teesside.

On 26 May 1917, a well-attended game between Bolckow Vaughan's (in 'dark blue jerseys and khaki pants') and Smiths Dock's (in 'light blue jerseys and light blue pants') Women Workers was played at South Bank football ground. The game, won by Bolckow's 2–1, was to raise funds for Hemlington Hospital, with several of the wounded soldiers sitting in the crowd enjoying the game.

The increased popularity of women's football across the region created great rivalry between the Tyne, Wear and Tees similar to that in the professional game. The top teams on Tyneside were: Blyth Spartans, North-Eastern Marine, Wallsend Slipway, Gosforth Aerodrome Aviation and Armstrong's Naval Yard. On Teesside there was: Bolckow's, Dorman's No 1, Darlington, Richardson-Westgarth No 1 & No 2, and Smith's Dock.

The games were 35 minutes long in each half. As interest increased, games took place in 1918 at St James' Park in Newcastle between teams representing the best players of Tyneside and Teesside. There was even a Tyne, Wear & Tees Munitionettes Challenge Cup, organised by the *Newcastle Daily Chronicle*, for thirty ladies' football teams. The competition was run on a north–south basis, with clubs in Teesside fighting it out to see which one of them would face the winner of the north section (i.e. clubs in the Newcastle area).

The first game in the Tees section was held on 13 October 1917 at Ayresome Park. Despite the poor weather, there was a large crowd to see Bolckow Vaughan and Dorman Long (Port Clarence) draw 1–1.

The two clubs who reached the final in 1918 were Blyth Spartans Munitions Girls from the northern section and Bolckow Vaughan Ladies, from the southern section. The first game, at St James' Park, ended

An advertisement for two important women's football games at Ayresome Park, Middlesbrough, in May 1918. Over 22,000 attended the Cup Final replay. (Courtesy of the Evening Gazette, Middlesbrough)

Right: *One of the first 'official' women's football games took place on 26 May 1917, to raise funds for Hemlington Hospital. (Courtesy of the* Evening Gazette, *Middlesbrough)*

SPORTS GAZETTE SATURDAY, MAY 26. 1917.

UNIQUE FOOTBALL MATCH.

BOLCKOW VAUGHAN'S v. SMITH'S DOCKS WOMEN WORKERS.

HANDSOME SUM RAISED

FOR BENEFIT OF WOUNDED AT HEMLINGTON HOSPITAL.

Left: *Action from the football game between Bolckow Vaughan and Smith's Dock ladies teams on 26 May 1917. (Courtesy of the* Evening Gazette, *Middlesbrough)*

0–0 before a crowd of 15,000 fans and the replay was played at Ayresome Park on Whit Saturday, 18 May 1918, with a bumper bank holiday crowd of 22,000 fans watching the game. Bolckow's won the toss and kicked off, but from the start there was no competing with Blyth Spartans – easily the best team in the region. Bolckow's star player, Winnie McKenna, was cheered every time she got the ball, but Spartans star, Bella Reay – one of the top players in the region – was on fine form, scoring a hat trick, and Bolckow Vaughan lost 5–0. Marty Lyons, who scored the fifth goal, was only aged 14!

Table 4: Industry in the Middlesbrough area 1914–19

Company/Firm/ Works	Type of Product	Total (tons)	Other Comment
Bell Brothers Ltd	Iron works – pig iron	1,226,717	3,086,185 tons coal, 3,492,736 tons Ironstone, 789,003 tons limestone also produced.
Bolckow, Vaughan & Co. Ltd	British/French shell steel Steel rails, sleepers, fish plates, bars for trench covers, shell forgings.	249,864 1,010,958	Total output 1,260,822 tons 5,700 employees enlisted (32.02 per cent of workforce) with 679 killed or missing (11.91 per cent).

Cochrane & Co. Ltd	Supplied cast iron pipes for Gretna Green, as well as Russia & France. Vast array of other steel products including cast iron pot liners for shell forgings.	n/a	458 employees enlisted.
Dorman, Long & Company Ltd	Iron & Steel Works Shell steel, shipbuilding material, rails & sleepers, ingot steel, pig iron, sheets, wire rod, barb & hawser, and 2,897,350 shell cases forging for shrapnel.	1,788,009 tons shell steel. 2,897,350 shell cases.	Britannia Works Clarence Works Redcar Works Bells, North-Eastern Steel Company Sir B. Samuelson Built new workshop at Britannia in February 1915. In Sept 1916, another workshop was built and run entirely by female labour – this produced shrapnel forgings for 18-pounder, and 18-pounder shells. Turned out 30–35,000 shell cases per week. 4,593 employees enlisted. Whole works placed at government's disposal. Extended plant at Redcar 1915. New works built at Tod Point Redcar, February 1916. Built new town called Dormanstown – 342 houses by 1918.
Furness Shipbuilding Co. Ltd	Shipbuilders (Works only started during war).	8 standard ships.	8 ships of 10,800 tons deadweight capacity built.
Gjers, Mills & Co. Ltd	Iron Works and shell makers.	Approx. 250,000 shells.	First shells accepted by government in October 1915. By July 1916 output 2,100 shells per week. In 1917 had to employ many women and output raised to 3,500 per week.

Heavy Stampings Ltd	Manufacturer of aero & ordnance materials.		Made aero engine parts, ordnance, & naval ordnance. Made tank parts & mechanical transport.
James & Ronald Ritchie	Acklam Foundry. Cast iron flange pipes/ connections for large explosive works.		Made 100 tons materials per week.
Joseph Constantine & Sons, of the Constantine & Pickering Steamship Co., Constantine & Donking S/S Co. & R.A. Constantine & Donking.	Ships	35 ships	Fleet of ships was all requisitioned at start of war for conveyance of naval & military stores & foodstuffs. 15 ships were sunk.
Richardson's, Westgarth & Co. Ltd	Marine Engine manufacturer.		Converted a number of machines to manufacture 4' lyddite shell bodies. Made machinery for destroyers, mine sweepers, trawlers, standard engines, metal mixers & other steel work. New workshop began in May 1915 to produce 6' & 8' high explosive shells.
Raylton, Dixon & Co. Ltd	Shipbuilders and ship repairers.	34 vessels made.	4 oil tankers 4 meat steamers 1 steamer – molasses 10 H.M. monitors 14 cargo steamers 1 passenger steamer Approx. 400 staff enlisted.
T. Roddam Dent & Son Ltd.	Shipped large quantities of explosives in form of benzole, naphtha, pig iron & shell steel. Iron ore, empty drums, foodstuffs & sundries discharged.	472,684 tons discharged & 211,344 tons shipped.	Most staff exempt from war, but six clerical staff and large number of crane workers, loco men and wharf labourers volunteered.

Teesside Bridge & Engineering Works Ltd	Manufacturer on government work. Made vast number of high explosive shells, shrapnel shells & bridges, barges, blast furnace & rolling mills, plant extensions, bridging equipment.		
Thos D. Ridley & Sons	Contractors. General construction work. Made shells.		Made 18-pounder shrapnel shells – made 202,000, and banded & loaded 350,000.
W Harkess & Son Ltd	Shipbuilders. Built ships & repaired ships.		Built 18 vessels. Repairs to 278 vessels. 76 staff enlisted. Visited by King & Queen 14 June 1917
Other Companies contributing included: **W Shaw & Co. –** Wellington Cast Steel Foundry **Skinningrove Iron Co. Stewarts Clothiers** (208,687 garments for military forces) **Sadler & Co. Ltd** (chemicals for explosives, creosote for Admiralty, tar distillers)			

'Give Us the Weapons'

Many companies in the area gave service to the war effort and Table 4 shows the wide range of vital products made during the war, signifying the crucial role of industry in Middlesbrough to winning the war.

This sheer determination is exemplified by the Gjers, Mills and Co. works which switched all of its production to munitions. Although not fully equipped to turn out shells, the manager of the Ayresome Iron Works, W. Chambers, took up the offer from T.D. Ridley to inspect their methods and, following discussions, led Gjers into production in 1915.

Women making munitions at the Gjers Mills & Co. Ayresome Ironworks, with the gentleman in charge casting a suspicious eye towards the camera. (Courtesy of the Dorman Museum)

One journalist wrote of the delicate touch used by women in the munitions factories when making shells, and women workers at Gjers demonstrate this for the camera. (Courtesy of the Dorman Museum)

On 2 December 1915, a crowd of 250 workers from all departments within Gjers gathered in the newly constructed shell shop to hear an address from Barnet Kenyon, MP for Chesterfield, appointed to visit and encourage munitions workers around the country. On the platform, which was draped with the Union Jack, were Mr L.F. Gjers, W. Chambers, works manager, and Mr Wallin, secretary. The workers at Gjers were praised, with thanks from the Ministry for their efforts and they, in turn, gave an assurance that they would continue to expedite production at the fastest rate possible. They eventually produced over 250,000 shells.

King George V passes the rivet store at Smiths Dock Company Ltd at South Bank on his visit there with Queen Mary on Thursday, 14 June 1917. (Courtesy of Middlesbrough Reference Library)

In recognition of the munitions work in the Middlesbrough area, King George V and Queen Mary visited the area on Thursday, 14 June 1917, along with Sir Eric Geddes, First Lord of the Admiralty, to 'inspect and encourage the work that was being done'.

The visit began at South Bank, with the royal couple being received by Sir Hugh Bell, Lord Lieutenant of the North Riding, and Lady Bell. They went first to Smith's Dock where

they met Chief Constable Henry Riches. Travelling on to Middlesbrough, they went to W. Harkess & Son, shipbuilders. The mayor and other dignitaries met the royal party at this point, and the visit included an inspection of ongoing work and a meeting between the king and their oldest employee, James Thom, who had been at the yard for sixty years. The queen received a bouquet from Nellie Pearson, the youngest of the female workers who, Her Majesty commented, were doing excellent service there. Another warm welcome awaited at Raylton, Dixon & Co. Ltd where they also met some local soldiers. Finally, they boarded the royal tug and during the journey to Stockton, Sir Hugh Bell pointed out the various factories they passed.

Most firms in the area found that they were very busy at the start of 1917. Business was generally prosperous, and relations between employer and employee were good. There was plenty of overtime work to meet the demand for products and many workers earned high wages. Although the various charities benefited from this, workers spent freely in other ways.

However, social conditions were still difficuly for many, with infant mortality still very high and older children considered to be getting out of control.

Alexandra Rose Day in 1915, with a group of young children standing in Newport Road ready to collect money for charity. (Courtesy of Teesside Archives)

Several events during the year attempted to address these issues, and bring much-needed fun to the town. Alexandra Rose Day in 1915 involved fund-raising as well as the holding of a large open-air whist drive along with various sports and a Market Gala Day.

On 9 February 1916, the mayor and mayoress in the Town Hall opened a Café Chantant, organised by the Women's Auxiliary of the Free Church of Middlesbrough. The slogan was 'come and enjoy a cup of tea as you listen to music, then see the art gallery'. It was said that the Town Hall 'presented a most cheery appearance, with numerous small tea tables … decorated with dainty tea equipages, … the cosy feeling augmented by the fragrant aroma of tea and coffee.' A sum of £200 was raised for the mayor's Central Relief Fund.

'Baby Week', originally scheduled for July but switched to October 1917 due to an outbreak of measles, proved a success giving many women the opportunity to seek advice regarding bringing up their children – particularly on health matters.

Friends in War

In Middlesbrough, two celebrations were held in 1918 to celebrate the link with Britain's allies: USA Independence Day on 4 July 1918 and French National Day on 14 July 1918.

Independence Day was marked by glorious sunshine and watched by large crowds gathered at the Town Hall to see Mayor J. Calvert review the American troops under the command of Lt Chesleigh Gray. They were entertained at the Town Hall before, at precisely 11 a.m., the troops, with Victoria Square behind them, marched up in front of the Town Hall. At their head was the 'Stars and Stripes'. To symbolise the US entry into the war, the troops carried in the centre of the ranks the first American flag to be shot down on the Western Front. The mayor gave a hearty welcome to the troops, praised President Wilson and pointed out to all that the Town Hall was also flying the 'Stars and Stripes'. The East Lancs band, which had been playing in Victoria Square, then played the 'Star Spangled

Banner' and the ceremony closed with three cheers for President Wilson. The US troops then marched down Albert Road, Newport Road, and Corporation Road ending up in front of the Middlesbrough Exchange.

Ten days later a similar event celebrated French National Day with a telegram being sent to the President of the French Republic followed by celebrations in the town, which resulted in a letter of thanks being received from the President.

Food for All

Maintaining adequate food supplies became more difficult in 1917 due to the increasing amount of shipping lost to German U-boat attacks. Following Local Government Board instructions on 2 August 1917, the Middlesbrough Local Food Control Committee was appointed on 13 August 1917, with Mayor J. Calvert in the chair.

All grocers and other sugar retailers were registered, following which there were two issues of sugar cards to the public – one was a family card and the other an individual card. For the local rationing scheme there were two issues of ration cards, and meat cards were also issued. Sugar was rationed in September 1917, and a scale of maximum charges for the sale of meat was fixed.

Close controls were maintained on commercial premises, particularly cafés. On 20 September 1917, a prosecution was successfully brought against the proprietor of the café at Marton Bungalow. Between 3 p.m. and 6 p.m. cafés were not allowed to sell more than 2oz of bread and cake for a meal. The inspector and his assistant had visited Marton Bungalow on 30 August and, having ordered two plain teas, had found their bread and cake to weigh 9.25 oz.

At the beginning of 1918, a draft rationing scheme had been prepared for tea, butter, margarine, lard and bacon. The food situation was becoming very critical, however, with long queues of up to 150m outside butcher shops. Margarine (or 'Maggie Ann' as they called it in Middlesbrough) was also in short supply.

MINISTRY OF FOOD.
CHILD'S RATION BOOK (A).

INSTRUCTIONS.

Read carefully these instructions and the leaflet which will be sent you with this Book.

1. The parent or guardian of the child named on the reference leaf as the holder of this ration book must sign his own name and write the child's name and address in the space below, and write the child's name and address, and the serial number (printed upside down on the back cover) in the space provided to the left of each page of coupons.

5 - OCT 1918

Food Office of Issue _____ Date _____

Signature of Child, Parent or Guardian } *Gertrude Hughes*

Name of Child *Alfred W. Hughes*

Address *6 Booth St Middlesbro*

2. For convenience of writing at the Food Office the Reference Leaf has been put opposite the back cover, and has purposely been printed upside down. It should be carefully examined. If there is any mistake in the entries on the Reference Leaf, the Food Office should be asked to correct it.

3. The book must be registered at once by the child's parent or guardian, who must take the book to the retailers with whom the child was previously registered for butcher's meat, bacon, butter and margarine, sugar and tea respectively, or, if the child has not previously held a book, to any retailers chosen. These retailers must write their names and the addresses of their shops in the proper space on the back of the cover. The books of children staying in hotels, boarding houses, hostels, schools and similar establishments should not be registered until they leave the establishment.

4. The ration book may be used only by or on behalf of the holder, to buy rationed food for him, or members of the same household, or guests sharing common meals. It may not be used to buy rationed food for any other persons.

[*Continued on next page.*

N. 1 (Nov.)

Vertical left margin: IF FOUND, RETURN TO AN ☀ FOOD OFFICE.

A child's ration book from October 1918. (Courtesy of the Dorman Museum)

Women queued from 5 a.m. at the doors of food shops, only to find that supplies quickly ran out when shops opened. Shops were empty by lunchtime and there were many, especially those employed in heavy industry, who felt that the food distribution system favoured residents living in the wealthier suburbs. On 17 and 18 January 1918, Chief Constable Henry Riches, who had been out among the queues, wrote that there was a great deal of dissatisfaction and 'some very nasty threats had been uttered'. Riches continued that 'he feared the present situation would bring about a cessation of work at many large works'. Urgent action was needed. The *North-Eastern Daily Gazette* stated that there was a 'grave situation at Middlesbrough … [with the public] beginning to display an ugly temper which will not brook many further disappointments'.

The following day, the situation got worse. A large number of workmen had marched on shops and demanded to be served with margarine. The situation in Newport Road turned so ugly that only the promise of an interview with the chief constable, and emergency supplies that afternoon, avoided hostile incidents. The Food Control Committee decided that they would commandeer all tea, butter and margarine coming into the town and distribute it using a ration ticket system. The new ration scheme was introduced that week. The *North-Eastern Daily Gazette* reported, on 22 January 1918, that the situation was calmer, with smaller queues and every household receiving a supply of margarine. The National Rationing Scheme eventually superseded the local committee.

A successful communal kitchen, organised by the Middlesbrough and District Women's Council, was opened at the back of Southfield Road on 7 November 1917. Between 700 and 800 portions were served each day. The Middlesbrough Food Control Committee also opened communal kitchens at the Old Police Station in the Market Place and in St Paul's Mission Hall, Cannon Street. Both were well patronised by local people, many of whom were among the poorest in the town.

THE MUNITIONS GIRLS

As well as being employed locally, girls went off to work in factories across the country, including Gretna Green and Hereford, two major munitions factories.

HM Factory Gretna was the UK's largest cordite factory, whilst the Rotherwas Factory at Hereford was the largest explosives filling plant in the country and employed nearly 6,000 people.

It was dirty and dangerous work – in one explosion at Hereford, twenty-nine workers died. An explosion in 1916 at Faversham, involving 200 tons of trini-trotoluene (TNT), killed 105 people, whilst seventy-nine died at Silvertown in West Ham, on 19 January 1917, when 50 tons of TNT exploded.

A journalist writing in the *North-Eastern Daily Gazette* gave an account of a visit to a munitions factory in 1916. He wrote that, because the women excel in work [requiring] great accuracy and delicate deftness of touch, the filling of the fuses had been left entirely in their hands. He paid tribute to the women workers as 'the work entails the handling of high explosives [and] the girls handle without a trace of nervousness, the deadly TNT and the even more deadly, fulminate of mercury'.

The theme continued with the mayor, Joseph Calvert, paying full tribute to 'the industry of the munitions workers who, having realised that munitions are vital to winning the war, have not shirked their duty [especially] women [undertaking] work to which they were altogether unaccustomed'.

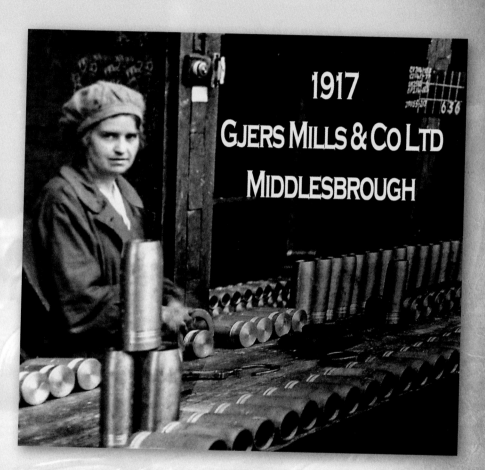

1917

GJERS MILLS & CO LTD

MIDDLESBROUGH

(Courtesy of the Dorman Museum)

6

'Dear Mother': News from the Front

One of the difficulties in writing this chapter was the enormity of material available. I decided that the hundreds of images and letters of the wounded or dead would be best represented through a 'pastiche' general impression of 'how it was for them'.

Getting the News

Contact with soldiers at the Front was always subject to censorship and the soldiers' desire not to alarm those back home. An official 'soldier's postcard' was printed in the *North-Eastern Daily Gazette* in late August to help people write a card meeting the approval of the censor. The sender was warned that if any sentences were used other than those on the card, the postcard would be destroyed.

The *North-Eastern Daily Gazette* reflected the increasing number of casualties with more and more news items about the individuals involved. The weekly *Sports Gazette* which carried the banner 'A Journal for All Manly Sports and Pastimes' had moved from carrying news of sporting events to reporting the war, its front and back pages full of images of the dead and wounded. The lists, and the photographs, increased as the major battles occurred. Occasionally the newspaper carried images found on the battlefield. One group of photos found in the mud of the Somme showed a young girl, and simply stated on the back Newport Road, Middlesbrough.

The first casualty lists began to be printed in the *North-Eastern Daily Gazette* in September 1914. One sad death was that of John Duncan Stubbs, from Nunthorpe. Aged only 15, he was a naval cadet on HMS *Aboukir*, one of three boats, along with HMS *Cressy* and HMS *Hogue*, torpedoed by a U-boat at 6.20 a.m. on the morning of 22 September. The incident, in which 1,459 men died, shocked the country. Stubbs, the son of the diarist solicitor Major Duncan Stubbs, had been a boarder at Coatham Grammar School, before going to Osborne College as a cadet. A memorial service was later held at Ormesby Parish Church at 5 p.m. on Friday, 2 October, and was attended by a large number of people.

Another service for all local men who had died (two from Middlesbrough and seven from Whitby) was held at the Church of the Missions to Seamen in Middlesbrough on 10 October. One local survivor was Leading Seaman Tom Galloway from North Ormesby who was on HMS *Cressy*. Galloway, who was in

By 22 May 1915, the Sports Gazette *had switched from front page images of sportsmen to photographs of those who had been killed or wounded, though it still called itself a 'Journal of all manly sports and pastimes'. (Courtesy of the Evening Gazette, Middlesbrough)*

John Bagley, from Middlesbrough, died when HMS Hampshire was sunk on 5 June 1916 and is shown here with one of his letters home. (Courtesy of the Dorman Museum)

the water for nearly three hours before being picked up by the Dutch steamer *Flora*, spoke of the horror of the scene and the bravery of the commander of the *Cressy*, the last to leave the ship.

A number of Teesside men were among the crew of HMS *Hampshire*, the ship carrying Lord Kitchener, which sank off the Orkney Islands on the evening of Monday, 5 June 1916. These included two stokers, John Bagley of Orwell St, Middlesbrough, and Joseph Dowson of Kings Road, North Ormesby, who were both aged 21.

In contrast, the tale of former Middlesbrough High School pupil, Maurice Myers, aged 17, had a happier ending. Arriving home at 'The Redlands', Linthorpe, in October 1915, he had been interned for a year at Ruhleben, following his arrest in 1914 whilst on holiday at Frankfurt. Maurice, who described life at the camp as being tedious rather than tough, was delighted to be home. There was also news of some other Teesside men interned at Ruhleben, when Middlesbrough Football Club received a letter from ex-player Jack Brearley, informing them that he was interned there along with ex-England and Middlesbrough stars, Fred Pentland and Steve Bloomer. He said they welcomed news of England – they were managing to get the football results, though they often arrived two weeks late.

A group of 'Boro-mad' soldiers, who called themselves the 'Tannerites', would have welcomed that news. The men, who were training at Camberley in England, thanked Middlesbrough Football Club for the football they had sent, the gesture having 'received a cheer so big you would have thought George Elliott [the club's English international forward] had scored a winning goal'.

Corporal Duncan McMaster of the Royal Flying Corps, who was shot down and interned at Griessen in Germany, wrote home that 'the camp was some change to the Borough, I can tell you'.

Trench Life

There were many other stirring stories. So many members of the Middlesbrough St Patrick's Club in Newport joined up that the club had to close.

Some families in Middlesbrough made remarkable contributions to the war effort. Mr and Mrs Myers of Walker Street, Newport, had seven sons serving in the army, whilst Thomas Flanagan of Duncombe Street had six sons on military service. The six Wallace brothers and their brother-in-law, as well as Rab, their pet spaniel, all went off to war. Astonishingly they all returned, even Rab the dog! Other examples include five men from the Dutton family of Camden Street, and four men from the Brough (Kent Street), Watson (Stansfield) and Atkinson families. Edith Thompson, sub-postmistress at The Bungalow, Ormesby, had her husband and two sons in the VTC and the army respectively.

Life in the trenches could be difficult. William Pennington of Newport Road, serving with the Scottish Borderers at the Front, wrote home describing life at the Front as 'hellish' and that the reality was beyond belief. He also wrote that anyone who was grumbling about the cost should come and see the misery here, and 'be grateful we were not the ones being invaded'.

Private Leonard Hindson, 2nd Grenadiers, arrived home to Redcar, after fighting at Mons and being injured by shrapnel during the retreat south from the Marne. Hindson, who described similar horrors, had been involved in the capture of 200 Germans, one of whom told him he had a wife in London.

Bombardier George Walker, a noted sprinter and secretary of Middlesbrough Harriers, died of shell-shock on 3 November 1917, after being brought home to a hospital in Shrewsbury.

A copy of a short letter home from the Front in October 1914 – the letter from a few 'Boro-ites' is a message to 'the Boro' to win the cup. (Courtesy of the Evening Gazette, Middlesbrough)

FROM THE FRONT.

October 1914 France

Dear Old Bird,

Best wishes from a few Boro.ites at the Front. Play up the Boro' and lift the Cup is our wish

John George Smith R.F.A. ('Late North Ormesby)

163

John Hunt, a teacher at Denmark St School, Middlesbrough, who was at the Front near Ypres with the 4th Yorks, wrote that even when they were in the rest trenches they were being shelled almost continuously.

The *North-Eastern Daily Gazette* carried several letters reflecting how difficult Christmas was for the men. Another letter described the famous 'Christmas Truce', with no firing at all after 6 p.m. on Christmas Eve through until Boxing Day. The letter also describes how men from both sides walked across no-man's-land to talk to each other and exchange gifts, and how the German trenches had Chinese lanterns all along the top of the parapet. One German, a waiter from London, said that the Germans did not want to fight. The letter concludes with 'I think he is telling the truth.'

It wasn't all gloom, however. A Middlesbrough soldier who was part of the British Expeditionary Force, describing his experiences going across to France, wrote that they had crossed to Boulogne on 14 August where they had received a very enthusiastic welcome from the French. Food and drink had been given

The six Wallace brothers, their brother-in-law, and Rab the spaniel, who all went to war and returned safely. (Courtesy of the Dorman Museum)

to them every step of the way from locals who just couldn't do enough to help them.

On 10 October, reports of the fall of Antwerp made the headlines, forcing the Belgian Government to move to France. Sixteen men from Middlesbrough, attached to the Marines, took part in the defence of Antwerp and all but one returned home safe. Another Middlesbrough soldier, Private Collett, wrote from his hospital bed at Battle in Sussex that he always looked forward to the *Sports Gazette*, and then proceeded to describe fighting on the Somme making it all sound like a football game.

> Soldiers at the front were supposed to spend four days in the front line, four days in support trenches, eight days in reserve trenches and then two weeks resting. Trenches could be up to 10ft deep, and quickly filled with water. Consequently many soldiers suffered from 'trench foot', a painful complaint where their feet literally rotted away. Over 80,000 soldiers are reputed to have suffered from shell-shock, though often this failed to be diagnosed.

On 6 October 1914 Eddy Blakiston wrote to his parents, John and Lilla, at 1 Willow Dene Terrace, Middlesbrough, from Antwerp to say that he had volunteered from his base at Chatham to go to Antwerp. He sailed across the Channel on HMS *Engadine*, landing at Ostend and going by train to Antwerp. Throughout the journey he received all sorts of goods – milk, cigarettes, silk handkerchiefs, cigars – and when they left the station all he could hear was 'Vive l'Anglais!' (England for ever!). They joined the Belgian soldiers and the next day they left in an armoured train for the Front. The scene of the fighting was one of devastation, with burning farmhouses and, when the nearby town (name unknown due to the censor) was in danger of falling, the Belgians burnt it down rather than let the Germans take it. Food was scarce; soldiers lived off the autumn fruit harvest, pears and a bit of hard bread. All Eddy possessed was a blanket and a spare shirt.

Another letter from Eddy Blakiston arrived on 13 October from '6 Armoured Train, Railway Station, Dunkirk'. He told how they had to evacuate from Antwerp, just making it over a bridge as it exploded and losing two of his comrades in the process. Despite the hardship of war, he described it as a thrilling experience when the French and Belgian soldiers fought, with each singing their national songs as they did so. He asked his parents to send him some 'Gold Flake … the fags here smell like fireworks.' He told more tales of the Belgians burning down their houses as they retreated rather than let the Germans take them. He ends his letter saying that, as he sleeps at night, he thinks of home scenes and faces and ends with 'God bless you and every one at home.'

One man who went to see for himself, describing it as a moment never to be forgotten, was the Rev. Beresford-Piers, Vicar of St John's Church, Middlesbrough. Through Sir Hugh Bell he managed to join the 4th Yorks, at the Front near Ypres, for two days in July 1915. He was able to deliver messages to the many local men in the battalion and later wrote to Mayor W.J. Bruce from Boulogne with a graphic description of the state of Ypres after heavy bombing.

Haringhe (Bandaghem) Military Cemetery in Belgium where Andy Jackson, captain of Middlesbrough Football Club in 1914, is buried. His grave is in the middle foreground. (Author's collection)

Many notable people from the town had their experience of war too. Lieutenant J.B.W. Pennyman, of the Kings Own Scottish Borderers, was reported missing after the Battle of Mons but was found to be safe a week later in early September. Captain L.C. Dorman, a nephew of Sir Arthur Dorman of Grey Towers, Nunthorpe, had been wounded with the BEF but was also safe.

Some well-known local men with Middlesbrough connections lost their lives in April 1915, including two solicitors, Captain John Nancarrow and Lieutenant Leonard I'Anson. Nancarrow practiced in Middlesbrough, and was very active in the town's Boy Scout movement, whilst Leonard I'Anson, having been articled with Jackson and Jackson of Middlesbrough, practiced in Saltburn. On 24 April 1915, Lt Erasmus Darwin, a member of the 4th Battalion Green Howards, and grandson of the great scientist Charles Darwin, also died. He had only been at the Front for a week when he was shot during the Battle of St Julien, part of the Second Battle of Ypres. Darwin and Nancarrow were close friends and are said to have been 'buried in one grave with a little cross over it, by a farmhouse, near St Julien'. Darwin had been employed as company secretary at Bolckow Vaughan's in Middlesbrough.

Many men had the *North-Eastern Daily Gazette* and the *Sports Gazette* sent out to them at the Front. Football dominated a lot of letters home, whether it was about the 'Boro' back home or football games the soldiers had played out there. There was one soldier who wrote that 'the war is OK, but sharing a trench with a Newcastle United fan is hard going'. Lots of other comments were made about the team's progress, individual players and games – it upheld morale during difficult times.

A Long Way from Ayresome

A number of staff from Middlesbrough Football Club served in the war, with several players being at the Front. Among those who lost their lives were club captain Andy Jackson, Harry Cook, Archibald Wilson, Dick Wynn and Don McLeod. Ex-club captain Robert Atherton, who had played for the Boro in the early 1900s (including the first ever League game at Ayresome Park), was killed at sea on 19 October 1917. John Harkins, Boro player 1906–08, also lost his life whilst serving in Iraq with the Black Watch in 1916.

Players returning from the war included Teesside Battalion men Joseph Hisbent and George Malcolm. Among those who returned to play again for the club after the war were Stewart Davidson, Walter Holmes (RAMC), Andy Wilson (6th Highland Light Infantry) and Walter Tinsley. Six of the aforementioned players, Jackson, Cook, Holmes, Davidson, Tinsley and Wilson, had all played in Boro's final League game at Blackburn, 24 April 1915, before League football closed down for the war. Remarkably Walter Tinsley, badly gassed in the trenches, who was one of Boro's final League goal-scorers in April 1915, scored Boro's first post-war goal at Sheffield Wednesday when League football returned on 30 August 1919.

An unusual encounter in September 1917 was described by a Boro fan in a letter home. One night, as a troop train going to the Front in Flanders pulled from the platform, a loud shout of: 'Hullo Stewart, how are ye?' came from a khaki clad figure waving his Balmoral cap, hanging halfway out of the window. 'Play up the Boro and the best of luck' yelled Stewart Davidson before the train vanished around a bend carrying Boro's centre forward, Andy Wilson.

Manager Tom McIntosh also joined the Teesside Battalion, serving as a sergeant on the Western Front. Several other staff worked in the local munitions industry. Vice Chairman Metcalf was in the National Reserve. Albert Forbes joined the Royal Artillery, being badly gassed in 1917. Other club directors joining up included J. Fowler who became a captain in the local Volunteer Force, whilst J. French and R. Turner were members of the Civil Guard, as was the club's assistant secretary. Sixteen gatemen were also in the local Volunteer Force or were members of the Civil Guard.

Don McLeod and Andy Jackson, Middlesbrough teammates from 1910 to 1913, both died in Belgium. McLeod was a gunner in the Royal Field Artillery, on 5 October 1917, when he was badly wounded, losing his right leg below the knee, as well as part of his other foot – catastrophic injuries for a footballer. It was a Boro fan, 'Gunner McEndoo' of Saltburn who helped stretcher his hero to a casualty clearing station, then later who wrote to the *Evening Gazette* with news of McLeod's terrible injuries. A *Gazette* reporter, on breaking the news to McLeod's wife and his three young daughters the next day, found she knew nothing about his death.

Andy Jackson was only 18 when he joined the club in 1910. He became club captain in Middlesbrough's glory days before the Great War. Jackson led by example and scored Boro's last goal before League football ended in a 2-2 draw away at Man United on 10 April 1915. Joining the Cameron Highlanders 5th Battalion, Jackson was stationed in the south of England, and made guest appearances for Chelsea before going out to Flanders, where he died on 30 September 1918 – only forty-one days before the war ended. The *Evening Gazette* 'Sunday War Special' on 13 October 1918 carried a headline, 'Sergeant "Andy" Jackson Killed', above a photo of him in full military regalia, and suggested every supporter would 'experience a sense of profound regret … that one of the most promising lads who ever donned the club's colours, has been killed'.

Middlesbrough Football Club player, Harry Cook, when he was a trainee teacher at North Ormesby Junior School. (Courtesy of the Dorman Museum)

The death of Jackson's teammate, 'Sergeant' Harry Cook, aged 23, was another tragic loss. Cook played for South Bank before making his debut for Middlesbrough at the age of only 18, in a 2–0 win at Derby in September 1912. As well as playing for Middlesbrough, Cook had worked as an uncertificated assistant master at North Ormesby Junior Boys' School since 7 October 1912. Here, the football hero taught the forty-three boys of Class IIIC. Although Cook joined the Teesside Battalion in January 1915, he continued to play for Middlesbrough for the rest of the season and, along with Jackson and Wilson, he played in Middlesbrough's final game at Blackburn before the club ceased playing football for the rest of the war. A letter from Harry Cook on 15 July 1916 describes life for him, and some of his Boro teammates, on the Somme. He wrote:

On one occasion the Huns lobbed a shell into the dugout where George Malcolm and several comrades had taken

Sunset at Grove Town Cemetery, Meaulte, in the Somme region, where the grave of Harry Cook is located. This remote rural setting is in contrast to the noise and mayhem which characterised the Somme region for much of the war. (Author's collection)

Thiepval Memorial is where another Middlesbrough Football Club player, Archibald Wilson, is remembered. One of 72,191 names of soldiers who were never found after the first day of the Battle of the Somme, 1 July 1916. (Author's collection)

THE NAMES OF 72,191 SOLDIERS WHO WERE NEVER FOUND ARE RECORDED HERE

THE SOMME ..... THIEPVAL MEMORIAL

cover. The Thornaby lad had a miraculous escape from death: he is still in the pink. Joe Hisbent, imperturbable Joe, has a good job; waiting for the Germans with a machine-gun. From my knowledge of the fair-haired Borough back he will stand firm as a rock against the best forward combination that the [Hun] can produce.

Six months later, in early January 1917, a sad letter from Cook's manager at Middlesbrough, Tom McIntosh, to the *North-Eastern Daily Gazette*, broke the news that Cook had been badly wounded after being hit by a shell fighting on the Somme. Cook never recovered, and died on 9 January 1917 leaving behind a wife and two children. Sadly, Cook had been accepted for a commission and was due to return to England three days later to begin officer training. Nearly a century later, he still rests in the isolated Grove Town Cemetery near Albert, a tranquil setting with fields stretching across gentle rolling hills to the distant Somme, far away from the noisy industrial landscape he had left behind. The words 'Yorkshire Regiment' are proudly displayed on his brilliant white headstone.

The Scot, Archibald Wilson, was killed at the Somme on 1 July 1916. Like Harry Cook, Wilson also played for Middlesbrough in 1914/15, in their final league season. With no known grave, his name is engraved among the thousands at Thiepval, the iconic memorial to the dead of that bloody day.

Dick Wynn, who scored on his debut for Middlesbrough in their 6-0 win against Tottenham Hotspur on 13 April 1914, was in the King's (Liverpool Regiment) and died on 11 April 1918 in Flanders. He is buried in Liverpool at the Anfield Cemetery and Crematorium.

The Middlesbrough Ambulance

One other member of Middlesbrough Football Club who contributed to the war effort was club chairman Phil Bach. He was part of the story of the 'Middlesbrough ambulance', a tale which reads almost like a *Boy's Own* adventure. When the British Red Cross called for more ambulances for the Front, Middlesbrough Borough Council decided to offer their new motor ambulance. With the vehicle costing £648 12*s* 4*d* (£648.62) the venture attracted huge local publicity. Former mayor, Alderman Alfred Mattison, aged 51, former player and chairman of Middlesbrough Football Club, and Phil Bach, ex-England International footballer and current Middlesbrough FC chairman, volunteered to drive the vehicle to the Western Front. An appeal was issued for donations of blankets, socks, knitwear and cigarettes to take with them. Tom McIntosh, the secretary of Middlesbrough FC, announced that the directors had purchased £5 worth of underclothing for the Middlesbrough ambulance to take to the Front; customers at the North Riding Hotel in Gurney Street, collected 550 cigarettes; whilst 5,000 cigarettes came from the employees of Dickson and Benson Ltd, the largest retailer in Middlesbrough, each packet carrying a message written by one of the firm's female employees.

Two weeks later, the dark green Austin motor ambulance, reg. DC 529, arrived and was displayed for two days at the Middlesbrough Fire Station. On the morning of Saturday

Alderman Alfred Mattison, on the left, and Phil Bach carrying out duties on the Western Front in autumn 1914. The injured soldier being stretchered has a German helmet placed on his body, whilst the Middlesbrough ambulance is behind them. (Courtesy of the Evening Gazette, Middlesbrough)

24 October the vehicle, with 'Middlesbrough Yorks' written on its side, pulled into the cobbled quadrangle in the middle of the Town Hall. A large crowd, enthralled by this heroic adventure, had gathered to see them leave. Led by the mayor, leading civic officials and many notable local sportsmen, they gave a hearty 'Three Cheers!' as the vehicle, laden with clothing and cigarettes, pulled away. Two days later, the directors of Middlesbrough FC in the minutes of their Board Meeting 'extended their heartiest appreciation … of the honourable duty the two men are undertaking'. Alfred's wife, Emily, received so many wishes of good luck on his behalf, that she issued a statement of thanks in the *North-Eastern Daily Gazette* on 31 October 1914.

After leaving Middlesbrough the men drove to London, staying in the Imperial Hotel whilst the ambulance was given its Red Cross logo and was altered to meet War Office requirements. The men finally headed to Folkestone on 29 October 1914, where they crossed the Channel to Boulogne. The ambulance was put straight to work, transporting the wounded from trains newly arrived from the Front to local hospitals and to the hospital ships. With each train carrying up to 400 men and over 3,000 casualties arriving in Boulogne each day, Mattison and Bach were kept busy. On 6 November 1914 under the command of commandant, Captain Kelly, RAMC, the Middlesbrough ambulance was sent to the Front as one of a convoy of fifteen vehicles joining No 2 Medical Army Corps.

Later, in a powerful recollection of their time in France, Mattison said that it was at this point that:

> They had their first real glimpse of war – the dead horse lying by the wayside, a crudely fashioned graveside, the intense booming of the guns, the passing of the refugees and the glare of burning homesteads.

The two men stayed in an old chateau, before finally moving to a local town. For a month the men, often under shellfire, transported the wounded from field hospitals to the clearing hospitals and the rail head for transportation to either Boulogne or Le Touquet. In his letters home, Mattison wrote that the Middlesbrough vehicle was much admired, but the roads were bad, with potholes 18in (0.45m) deep causing many vehicles to end up in roadside ditches. Although driving the vehicle was difficult (it weighed 2 tons, unladen) he would only bring the ambulance home when there were plenty of other vehicles to do the work.

Remarkably, they were sighted on at least two occasions. In a letter received on 30 November 1914 from Lance Corporal W. Danby of the Army Service Corps (Expeditionary Force) he described how he was:

> Passing a Red Cross hospital on Monday morning (23 November), fairly early, I saw the ambulances from which the wounded soldiers were being removed, when the words 'Middlesbrough, Yorks, stood out very prominently on one of the cars. At first I thought I was dreaming, but I soon came to my senses when I saw our worthy ex-Mayor superintending the careful removal of wounded soldiers and the managing director of the Boro' at the wheel. The handshake they gave me was rather nippy for a cold frosty morning but it was proof of their pleasure at seeing me.

Another sighting took place on 5 December 1914. Leonard Griggs, RAMC 23rd Field Ambulance, wrote to 'Old Bird' in the *North-Eastern Daily Gazette*'s *Sports Gazette* that he had just 'had the pleasure of meeting Phil Bach half an hour ago'.

At the end of November, with the conditions at the Front becoming increasingly muddy, it was becoming more apparent that the Middlesbrough ambulance was not suited to the conditions. Captain Kelly wrote to Mattison:

> I think it is a convenient time to return home. You have had a good deal of work and experience with your Ambulance, which is very comfortable, but I would advise you to bring a lighter and shorter M.A. Wagon if you think of coming out again.

Having driven back to Boulogne on 1 December 1914, Mattison was then asked by Mr Stanhope, director of transport to the British Red Cross, for the vehicle to be left in France since he thought it could be of further use. Leaving Bach behind as a spare driver, Mattison took a few days leave. He returned to France on 11 December 1914 to find that they were again required for duty. Two days later, the Middlesbrough ambulance began various duties in the Le Touquet and Boulogne area, including another spell at the Front with the No 2 Medical Army Corps, transporting the wounded from field hospitals.

THE POWER OF THE PRESS

The press, with their political allegiances, were an influential power. For most people it was their main source of news, with people queuing to buy the latest edition in an attempt to keep up with the latest developments. Middlesbrough's daily newspaper, the *North-Eastern Daily Gazette*, with a certified daily circulation of over 70,000 copies, was a leader in keeping local pople informed of events. With its support for the Liberal government, the paper was strongly anti-war until the last few days of peace.

The *North-Eastern Daily Gazette* was one of the first provincial papers in the country to launch a special Saturday sports edition in the 1890s. The 'journal of all manly sports and pastimes' carried reports and illustrations of Middlesbrough's latest match. Pioneering *Gazette* sports editor, W.J. Gill, wanted to make it bigger, better and more influential than the publications already available in Newcastle and Manchester, which were simply updated editions of that day's newspaper.

During the war the *Sports Gazette* had a dual function. It carried, every week, images of those who had died or were wounded, and it was also very popular with the soldiers themselves fighting at the Front. There were many letters from the men, talking warmly about their pleasure at receiving the latest copy of the *Sports* from home.

Sadly, the shortage of paper had an adverse effect on the paper in the last year of war and it was reduced to a tabloid edition, with only generic sports news, rather than the vibrant link to home it had once been.

(*Evening Gazette*, *Middlesbrough*)

PRIVATE JAMES SMITH. V.C.

Private James Smith, the first recipient from Middlesbrough of the Victoria Cross for bravery shown in action in December 1914. (Courtesy of the Dorman Museum)

Bach wrote home just before Christmas to say that he was well, and that he was 'quite enjoying the experience [and] would not have missed it for anything'. The two men spent Christmas 1914 on duty in France, but on 31 December with the Red Cross having declared they had enough vehicles, and driving conditions in France becoming increasingly difficult, Mattison decided to return home. He had heard about the bombardment of Hartlepool, and thought the ambulance would be needed for more urgent duties back in Middlesbrough. Mattison drove back to Boulogne en route for England, where he arrived on 5 January 1915. Having taken personal responsibility for returning the vehicle in a state fit for future use, Mattison must have been somewhat relieved to arrive back in Middlesbrough.

Two letters of commendation were received from senior British Red Cross officials regarding the work carried out by Bach and Mattison. Whilst Mattison remained active in the war effort in Middlesbrough, Phil Bach, having joined another convoy, served in France and Egypt, before returning in April 1916. A minute at the Middlesbrough Football Club board meeting on 8 May 1916, records 'the Members of the Board expressed their great pleasure on having the Chairman with them and congratulate him on … his safe return.' In June 1918 he enlisted again as a captain in the Shropshire Yeomanry, before finally returning to Middlesbrough in early December 1918.

Middlesbrough VC's

Two men from Middlesbrough were awarded the Victoria Cross. They were Private James Smith of 3rd Battalion Border Regiment but attached to the 2nd Border Regiment, and Private Tom Dresser of D Company, 7th Yorkshire Regiment (Alexandra, Princess of Wales' Own).

Smith, aged 33, was a reservist at the start of the war. He received his award for twice helping to rescue wounded men whilst under fire at Rouge Bancs, near Neuve Chappelle, on 21 December 1914. He was described as an unassuming man who came from Cumbria, but was working at Normanby Iron Works when he was called up. Smith was wounded in March 1915, and returned to Middlesbrough to convalesce. He was given several receptions in his honour including being guest of honour at a recruitment meeting for the Teesside Battalion in April 1915, at Middlesbrough Town Hall where the mayor gave him a special presentation. In return, Smith made an emotional 'thank you' to the town and, although he was from the north-west, said he hoped to return to Middlesbrough once the war was over. He did return, and died in the town in 1968.

In 1917, Private Tom Dresser became the second man from the town to be awarded the Victoria Cross after his brave actions at the Front. (Courtesy of the Dorman Museum)

Dresser, aged 25, won his VC on 12 May 1917, close to Roeux where, despite being injured twice, he succeeded in conveying an important message from battalion headquarters to front line trenches. On his eventual return to Middlesbrough on the evening of Saturday, 17 September 1917, Dresser was given a hero's welcome. Expecting Dresser on the 7.32 p.m. train from Manchester, a huge crowd, including the mayor and civic officials, awaited him. When the train arrived empty, the crowd was forced to wait. Dresser eventually arrived forty minutes later, totally unaware of the welcoming party. As he stepped out of the carriage the band struck up 'See the Conquering Hero Comes'. After meeting civic officials, Dresser eventually got to embrace his mother. Cheered by the crowds all the way, Dresser joined the mayor in an open top procession to the Town Hall, where he appeared on the steps to face an ovation from several thousand people. After a presentation of a small token from the mayor, Dresser was too full to reply, but he made known that he was proud of the welcome. The evening ended with 'three cheers!' for Dresser and his parents. Dresser also returned to live in Middlesbrough, until his death in 1982.

A GROUP OF MARTON HALL BOYS IN FRANCE.

Standing (left to right): Sappers, DODSWORTH, POULE, PROUD, RYMER, FOX, BAILES, SPRUCE,
Sitting (left to right): Corpl. HARLEY, Sergt. DEAN; Lance-Corpl. NORTH.

A group of soldiers in France on 5 May 1917, all of whom completed training at Marton Hall. (Courtesy of the Evening Gazette, Middlesbrough)

Teesside Battalion in France

The Teesside Battalion arrived in France on 2 June 1916. Although they were primarily there as a pioneer battalion, a role that they were thrown into only a few days after arriving, despite having no training or preparation for the Front, the battalion did see action on several occasions.

The first death occurred on 30 June 1916, when Private John Latimer, aged 24, was killed. The first officer to be killed was Lt Henry Bloom, aged 25. He was killed on 14 February 1917 by a 5.9 shell in Abode Lane, a forward communication trench where he was in charge of a working party. A former pupil of Middlesbrough High School, Bloom was the sixth solicitor with Middlesbrough connections to have died at that time – the others being Captains Bowes-Wilson, Nancarrow, I'Anson and 2nd Lts Hutchinson and Ewart Richardson. The latter, aged 35, was killed in action on 27 September 1916.

After seeing action throughout 1917 and into 1918, the battalion suffered particularly heavy casualties in April 1918. When the 40th Division was reconstituted, the 17th Worcestershire Regiment became the pioneer battalion and the 12th Battalion Yorkshire (Teesside Pioneers) was absorbed as part of the 17th Worcestershire, with effect from 28 June 1918. The Teesside Battalion was no more.

Little Billy from Middlesbrough

One of the more unusual aspects of life at the Front was the column written by Major Jack Fairfax Blakeborough, an expert horseman and member of the literary staff at the *North-Eastern Daily Gazette*.

Fairfax Blakeborough served as a major in the 15th/19th King's Royal Hussars, and was awarded the Military Cross.

As a writer, Fairfax Blakeborough brought a sense of light humour to war reports with his accounts of imaginary tales of Teesside characters at the Front. Based on his impeccable knowledge of the Middlesbrough area, they were very popular among *North-Eastern Daily Gazette* readers. In his biography, Fairfax Blakeborough says that when he began his weekly articles 'he received shoals of letters from home'. He explained that his object was to 'give some comfort to the mothers of serving men and to show that we had some fun in France and that all was not quite as sordid as they imagined'.

He had great admiration for the British soldier, and loved the humour of the men from Teesside. Regular articles from Fairfax Blakeborough began in October 1917 under the title 'A Few Chirps from France.' His weekly articles often featured 'Little Billy from Middlesbrough' and, with his ability to bring the character alive allied with his acquaintance of military life, he made real to readers the world of the homesick Middlesbrough soldier serving at the Front. They were a mixture of fine detail of life in France and self-effacing humour about life back in Stockton or Middlesbrough.

The lads out in France were always reminiscing about home, and wondering what was happening down at Middlesbrough Market on a Saturday night. Remarkably the soldiers out at the Front were able to enjoy the columns when they received their copies of the *Sports Gazette* from home. A letter from France, from 'Nine Boroughites' on 17 November 1917, comments that 'we all enjoy old Blakey's notes, they seem to get better all the time'.

Some of his best work came in the articles written at Christmas as he describes a frosty winter morning at the Front when 'one longs for the unmarred beauty of Cleveland, the grandeur of her hills, the sounds and scents of her farms. Looking out across the frozen trenches, Little Billy thinks only of skating at Billingham Bottoms and walking down Linthorpe Road.' It was the ability to bring the trenches into the homes of people back in England that made the work of Fairfax Blakeborough so special.

A Gallant and Competent Officer

It is impossible to come even close to mentioning all of those who were wounded or died in the war. There are so many stories that it would be beyond the realms of several books to even begin to give coverage to their experiences. However, there is perhaps need to mention just one more:

This book began with a description of the opening of the new bowling green at Albert Park, the last municipal duty of George Bowes-Wilson. Although letters continued to be received from him in May 1915, Bowes-Wilson was reported on 25 May 1915 as suffering from the effects of being gassed, and was said to be in 'a terrible state'. On 17 June 1915, Bowes-Wilson was killed outside his dugout in Sanctuary Wood by a German sniper. On hearing of his death, Gertrude Bell described Bowes-Wilson as a 'most gallant and competent officer'.

He is buried at Vlamertinghe Military Cemetery, 5km west of Ypres. A written description of his burial survives, and a moving extract from this is given below – a fitting way to end this book:

Shortly before mid-day, the remains of Captain George Bowes-Wilson were laid in their last resting place in a peaceful spot near the ruins of ---- Church. It was a solemn party, which took the body from the camp of the 4th York. Regiment (where it had been brought the night before from the trenches) ... the small party stood round the open grave and heard the beautiful burial service of the Church of England read by the chaplain of the 150th Brigade, the Rev. Mr Birch of Darlington.

Very few eyes looked on that were not dim with tears ... the grave is marked with a rough wooden cross and two beautiful wreaths made from simple wild flowers were placed on it as a token of esteem ... whilst the burial service was being conducted the roar of the guns could be heard in the distance. It was truly the funeral of a soldier, simple yet impressive ...'

Postscript

Peace at Last

The war came to an end on 11 November 1918. In Middlesbrough, the day, which had been widely anticipated, brought widespread celebrations. The *North-Eastern Daily Gazette* describes it:

> The rejoicings ... continued without interruption till nearly midnight and the town has seldom passed through fourteen hours of such joy. In the afternoon the streets were a seething mass of humanity and Linthorpe Road has seldom been so congested.

Schools and factories had closed by midday as people continued to pour into the centre of town. Despite the celebrations being subject to the wartime restrictions still in effect, the *North-Eastern Daily Gazette* reported that:

> The sky was lit up at intervals by the pyrotechnic display ... [the town] may never again have an occasion when the circumstances so thoroughly justified such an explosion of pent-up exuberant patriotic feelings.

The climax of the day came when Mayor J. Calvert read out the official announcement of the Armistice from the Town Hall balcony in Corporation Road, which was 'a perfect sea of human faces'. The excited crowds heard the mayor say that never before had a mayor been called upon to make a declaration so momentous,

The North-Eastern
Daily Gazette
announces the
end of the war on
11 November 1918.
(Courtesy of the
Evening Gazette,
Middlesbrough)

and one which contained for the people so much cause for joy and gladness. A procession took place involving civic officials, representatives of the military, and members of the church, and Milburn's Band led the singing of the doxology and the Rev. J.T. Brown pronounced the benediction. The mayor declared a holiday for all schoolchildren the next day, and he hoped businesses would follow suit. All recruiting was suspended at the Military Service Tribunal.

The editorial in the *North-Eastern Daily Gazette* gives a reminder of the sacrifice of war:

> We must not overlook the steadfastness of the soldiers … all our joy must be tempered by remembrance of the stupendous sacrifice entailed … if the millions who have fallen to rise no more, could be made to stand at ease they would stretch from John O'Groats to Land's End.

On Sunday, 17 November 1918, a formal thanksgiving was held at Middlesbrough Town Hall, which was filled to capacity. The *North-Eastern Daily Gazette* described the gathering as 'one of the most remarkable in the town's history representing, as it did, every phase of religious opinion'. The following day a 'Thank the Guns' campaign was formally opened. The centrepiece for this, in the area around the Bolckow Statue close to the Exchange building, was a recreation of a ruined Belgian house, surrounded by howitzers, guns of all kinds, sand-bagged trenches and a mobile pigeon loft. The opening ceremony included a procession led by the mayor, from the Town Hall to the display, where the Union Jack was broken and the national anthem was sung. Schoolchildren marched in procession, and many who had bought Savings Certificates and War Bonds gave them to the mayoress to publicly burn. The gesture pleased Middlesbrough Borough Council so much that every child was sent a beautiful card as a memento of the historic occasion.

However, the influenza epidemic had brought sadness to the town in the autumn of 1918. The death rate tripled for October and November, with 200 deaths from influenza and 130 from pneumonia in one month. Coming so soon after the ravages of war, this was a difficult time for many.

The following summer, on 19 July 1919, a celebration 'Peace Day' was held. The ringing of the bells of St Hilda's Church in the old town at 9 a.m. summoned the people to rejoice. Crowds were already out in the streets. The Victory March began with the presentation of the colours of the 9th Yorkshire Battalion to the mayor at the Town Hall. The procession of civic officials, representatives of the armed forces and many other agencies that had contributed to the war effort, went first to the site of the tank in Park Road South, where the Corporation received the 'engine of war'. Then they went to Albert Park, where H.W.F. Bolckow planted a tree to commemorate the 50th anniversary of the opening of Albert Park (this had been held over from the previous year). In the afternoon there were further celebrations, including

The official announcement of the Armistice is made at Middlesbrough Town Hall on 12 November 1918. (Courtesy of the Dorman Museum)

Many types of memorials were produced in the immediate war years as communities commemorated their war heroes, including this roll of honour from Cannon Street. (Courtesy of the Dorman Museum)

a cycle parade and carnival; a horse parade, grand gymkhana and sports (at Ayresome Park); a grand gala in the Market Place – which went on till dusk – a display of boxing by boys from the Industrial School; a water carnival and other entertainments in Albert Park to complete the day. To complete the peace celebrations, a united service was held the following Sunday afternoon at the Town Hall.

After the war, the people of villages, towns and cities across Britain marked the huge loss of life by setting up a large number of buildings, monuments, stained glass windows and plaques as memorials.

The question of an appropriate memorial to those who had given their lives had been broached in the *North-Eastern Daily Gazette* the day after the signing of the Armistice. Middlesbrough's War Memorial Committee found it very difficult to decide how to honour the town's dead. It wasn't just the challenge of finding the money; opinion in the town was divided between a traditional memorial and the provision of leisure or medical facilities that would be of long lasting benefit to those left behind. The decision to erect a monument was made at a public meeting in October 1919.

The Peace Celebrations, which were held on 19 July 1919, began with the presentation of the colours of the 9th Yorkshire Battalion at the Town Hall. (Author's collection)

One of the many celebration events held in July 1919. (Author's collection)

The idea originally came from George W. Forrester, Kelling Sanatorium, Norfolk, an ex-soldier who had lived in Middlesbrough. He suggested displaying the war trophies presented to the town, with a monument erected close by, and that a fund should be opened to finance this.

Progress was slow. Walter Brierley, a York architect, was invited to submit designs but these were rejected as being too elaborate and expensive. The committee wanted a simpler design, and finally approved a proposal from Sir Arthur Dorman for a cenotaph erected on a site that he had donated, close to the Dorman Museum and Albert Park. With a public appeal fund in place, construction finally began in April 1922 under a barrage of criticism that the War Memorial Committee had spent far too much time in discussion.

The Gjers roll of honour commemorating all of their workers who joined up during the war. (Courtesy of the Dorman Museum)

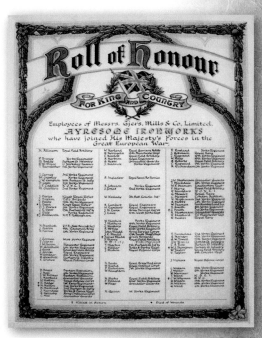

Middlesbrough's war memorial, a cenotaph more than 10m high, was unveiled on 11 November 1922 in memory of more than 3,000 local men who had died in the First World War. Built at a cost of £17,000, the cenotaph of Aberdeen granite stands outside the entrance gates to Albert Park. A new wall of Portland stone with wrought iron gates was also erected. Attached to the walls are bronze panels inscribed with the names of those who died.

On Saturday, 11 November 1922, a military and civilian procession, including Middlesbrough's two VCs, Privates James Smith and Tom Dresser, marched along a crowded route from the Town Hall. At 11 a.m. the deputy mayor, J.G. Pallister, unveiled the cenotaph and two blinded soldiers, Lt J. Swales and Private G. Hollins unveiled the inscribed bronze tablets, whilst Private Dowson, Middlesbrough's first blinded soldier,

The memorial is unveiled, watched by large crowds. (Courtesy of the Dorman Museum)

After the ceremonial part of the day, crowds watched ex-servicemen as they filed past the memorial, many of them wearing their medals from the conflict. (Courtesy of the Dorman Museum)

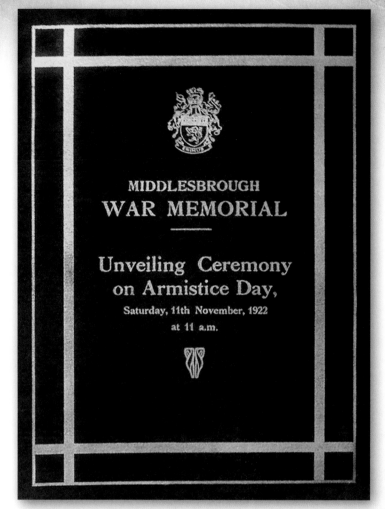

MIDDLESBROUGH
WAR MEMORIAL

Unveiling Ceremony
on Armistice Day,

Saturday, 11th November, 1922
at 11 a.m.

The town's official memorial to those who had died was unveiled on 11 November 1922, and marked by this commemorative booklet. (Courtesy of the Dorman Museum)

opened the new Park gates. The Green Howards sounded the 'Soldier's Farewell', three rounds were fired before reveille and finally the national anthem.

Now the town could begin to go forward again, and look toward the future years. One war was over but, for many who had been through it, a much longer conflict was beginning as they tried to put their lives back together and move on.

BIBLIOGRAPHY AND SOURCES

A wide range of sources have been consulted and the following is an overview of these:

Private Papers

Bach, Phil
Bell-Moulang, F.
Hustler, William H.
Kirby, R.L.

Nielsen, G.
Pennyman, J.W.
Stubbs, Thomas Duncan
Warne, K.

Other Sources

British Red Cross War Reports: North Riding 1914–1920.
Hansard Parliamentary Proceedings, 1914–1918.
Middlesbrough Borough Council minutes & accounts, 1876–1924.
Middlesbrough Education Committee minutes, 1913–1918.
Middlesbrough Football Club minutes and accounts for 1913–1920.
Middlesbrough Guardians minutes, 1913–1919.
North-Eastern Daily Gazette, 1913–1924.
Northern Echo, 1914–1918.
North Riding Infirmary records for North Ormesby &
    Hemlington Hospitals.
Oral testimonies of over 250 individuals from the period.
Recruitment documents regarding recruitment in Middlesbrough,
    and the formation of the Teesside Battalion, including leasing of
    Marton Hall.
School log books for many schools in the Middlesbrough area.
Stockton Rural Council minutes, 1913–1918.
Teesside Battalion War Diary 1918.

Unpublished: Osborne, J. (ed.), 'History of the Bank of England 1914–1926', archive catalogue ref. M7/156–159.
Unpublished: 'Study of an Unofficial Pals Battalion', Peter Thomas, 2007.
War cemeteries and museums in Ypres, Belgium and the Somme region France.

Books on the Period

Mitchinson, K.W., *Pioneer Battalions of the Great War*, Pen & Sword, 1997.
Powell, G., *The History of the Green Howards*, Casemate, 2002.
Sheen, J., *Durham Pals*, Pen & Sword, 2006.
Sutherland, J. and D. Canwell, *Battle of Britain 1917*, Pen & Sword, 2006.
Westlake, R., *The Territorials 1908–1914*, Pen & Sword, 2013.

ABOUT THE AUTHOR

Paul Menzies has been writing about North East England since 1985 and is the author of a number of local history books. He has worked with the BBC on many occasions, including the series *Keep the Home Fires Burning* which he wrote and presented in August 2014. Paul was historical consultant for Granada Television on *In Suspicious Circumstances*. He also contributed to the British Film Institute's (BFI) Mediatheque project for North East England in 2010 and is currently part of the team working on the 'Middlesbrough in the Great War' exhibition for the Dorman Museum, Middlesbrough.

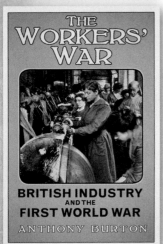